Contents

Licence

Text © Pat Hoodless
© 2003 Scholastic Ltd

Published by Scholastic Ltd, Villiers House,
Clarendon Avenue, Leamington Spa,
Warwickshire CV32 5PR

Printed by Bell & Bain Ltd, Glasgow

4 5 6 7 8 9 0   5 6 7 8 9 0 1 2

British Library Cataloguing-in-Publication Data
A catalogue record for this book is available from
the British Library.

ISBN 0-590-53476-9

**Visit our website at
www.scholastic.co.uk**

CD developed in association with
Footmark Media Ltd

Author
Pat Hoodless

Editor
Christine Harvey

Assistant Editors
Dulcie Booth and
Roanne Charles

Series Designer
Joy Monkhouse

Cover photographs
© Photodisc,
© Sheila Hogbin,
© Science and Society
Picture Library,
© Stockbyte.

Acknowledgements

Thanks to Sheila Hogbin for her involvement with the interviews.

Extracts from the National Curriculum for England © Crown copyright material is
reproduced with the permission of the Controller of HMSO and the Queen's Printer for
Scotland.

Every effort has been made to trace copyright holders and the publishers apologise for
any omissions.

List of resources on the CD-ROM

The page numbers refer to the teacher's notes provided in this book.

INTRODUCTION

This book and CD-ROM support the teaching and learning set out in the QCA Scheme of Work for History in Year 1. The CD provides a large bank of visual and oral resources. The book provides teacher's notes, background information, ideas for discussion and activities to accompany the CD resources, along with photocopiable pages to support the teaching. All have been specifically chosen to meet the requirements for resources listed in the QCA units on toys, homes and holidays. Additional resources have also been included to enable teachers to broaden these areas of study if they wish to, such as stories and personal accounts. The resources are also relevant and useful to those who may not be following the QCA Schemes, particularly teachers in Scotland.

The resources and activities are not intended to be used rigidly, however, since they do not provide a structure for teaching in themselves. The teacher's notes provide ideas for discussion and activities which focus on the 'Knowledge, skills and understanding' of the National Curriculum for history. They aim to guide teachers in developing the children's skills and concepts fundamental to early understanding of what it is to learn about the past. The focus is on developing the children's awareness of similarity and difference, sequencing, understanding chronology, questioning and investigating historical sources and communicating findings in a variety of ways. Above all, the activities and discussions aim to build clear links between the children's own real-life experiences and their developing awareness of the past.

Links with other subjects

Literacy
There are a number of close links between the topics covered in this book and work on literacy. The discussion activities contribute directly to the requirements for speaking and listening. The stories may be used in shared reading during the Literacy Hour, or to provide a stimulus for shared, guided or independent writing. Similarly, the writing frames may be used to support guided or independent writing. Pictures from the CD could be printed to stimulate independent writing or to illustrate it.

Art and design
There are close links with art and design. Much work at Key Stage 1 needs to be visual. Wherever possible, therefore, activities in the teacher's notes are based on visual sources and make extensive use of drawing to extend the children's own understanding of a particular topic or concept. For example, in drawing pictures comparing old and new toys, the children are required to represent their own understanding of that concept.

Design and technology
The content of the 'Toys' and 'Homes' chapters, relates closely to technological developments. For example, the discussion and work children will carry out on remote-controlled toys relates closely to this area of the curriculum and will enhance their understanding of modern technologies and how they work.

HOW TO USE THE CD-ROM

Windows NT users
If you use Windows NT you may see the following error message: 'The procedure entry point Process32First could not be located in the dynamic link library KERNEL32.dll'. Click on **OK** and the CD will autorun with no further problems.

Setting up your computer for optimal use
On opening, the CD will alert you if changes are needed in order to operate the CD at its optimal use. There are three changes you may be advised to make:

Viewing resources at their maximum screen size
To see images at their maximum screen size, your screen display needs to be set to 800 x 600 pixels. In order to adjust your screen size you will need to **Quit** the program.

If using a PC, open the **Control Panel**. Select **Display** and then **Settings**. Adjust the **Desktop Area** to 800 x 600 pixels. Click on **OK** and then restart the program.

If using a Mac, from the **Apple** menu select **Control Panels** and then **Monitors** to adjust the screen size.

Adobe Acrobat Reader
To print high-quality versions of images and to view and print the photocopiable pages on the CD you need **Adobe Acrobat Reader** installed on your computer. If you do not have it installed already, a version is provided on the CD. To install this version **Quit** the 'Ready Resources' program.

If using a PC, right-click on the **Start** menu on your desktop and choose **Explore**. Click on the + sign to the left of the CD drive entitled 'Ready Resources' and open the folder called 'Acrobat Reader Installer'. Run the program contained in this folder to install **Adobe Acrobat Reader**.

If using a Mac, double click on the 'Ready Resources' icon on the desktop and on the 'Acrobat Reader Installer' folder. Run the program contained in this folder to install **Adobe Acrobat Reader**.

PLEASE NOTE: If you do not have **Adobe Acrobat Reader** installed, you will not be able to print high-quality versions of images, or to view or print photocopiable pages (although these are provided in the accompanying book and can be photocopied).

QuickTime
In order to view the videos and listen to the audio on this CD you will need to have **QuickTime version 5 or later** installed on your computer. If you do not have it installed already, or have an older version of **QuickTime**, the latest version is provided on the CD. If you choose to install this version, **Quit** the 'Ready Resources' program.

If using a PC, right-click on the **Start** menu on your desktop and choose **Explore**. Click on the + sign to the left of the CD drive that is entitled 'Ready Resources' and open the folder called 'QuickTime Installer'. Run the program contained in this folder to install **QuickTime**.

If using a Mac, double click on the 'Ready Resources' CD icon on the desktop and then on the 'Acrobat Reader Installer' folder. Run the program contained in this folder to install **QuickTime**.

PLEASE NOTE: If you do not have **QuickTime** installed you will be unable to view the films.

Menu screen
▶ Click on the **Resource Gallery** of your choice to view the resources available under that topic.
▶ Click on **Complete Resource Gallery** to view all the resources available on the CD.
▶ Click on **Photocopiable Resources (PDF format)** to view a list of the photocopiables provided in the book that accompanies this CD.
▶ **Back**: click to return to the **opening screen**. Click **Continue** to move to the **Menu screen**.
▶ **Quit**: click **Quit** to close the menu program and progress to the **Quit screen.** If you quit from the **Quit screen** you will exit the CD. If you do not quit you will return to the **Menu screen**.

Resource Galleries
▶ **Help**: click **Help** to find support on accessing and using images.
▶ **Back to menu**: click here to return to the **Menu screen**.
▶ **Quit:** click here to move to the **Quit screen** – see **Quit** above.

Viewing images

Small versions of each image are shown in the Resource Gallery. Click and drag the slider on the slide bar to scroll through the images in the Resource Gallery, or click on the arrows to move the images frame by frame. Roll the pointer over an image to see the caption.

▶ Click on an image to view the screen-sized version of it.

▶ To return to the Resource Gallery click on **Back to Resource Gallery**.

Viewing videos

Click on the video icon of your choice in the Resource Gallery. In order to view the videos on this CD, you will need to have **QuickTime** installed on your computer (see 'Setting up your computer for optimal use' above).

Once at the video screen, use the buttons on the bottom of the video screen to operate the video. The slide bar can be used for a fast forward and rewind. To return to the Resource Gallery click on **Back to Resource Gallery**.

Listening to sound recordings

Click on the required sound icon. Use the buttons or the slide bar to hear the sound. A transcript will be displayed on the viewing screen where appropriate. To return to the Resource Gallery, click on **Back to Resource Gallery**.

Printing

Click on the image to view it (see 'Viewing images' above). There are two print options:

Print using Acrobat enables you to print a high-quality version of an image. Choosing this option means that the image will open as a read-only page in **Adobe Acrobat** and in order to access these files you will need to have already installed **Adobe Acrobat Reader** on your computer (see 'Setting up your computer for optimal use' above). To print the selected resource, select **File** and then **Print**. Once you have printed the resource **minimise** or **close** the Adobe screen using — or **X** in the top right-hand corner of the screen. Return to the Resource Gallery by clicking on **Back to Resource Gallery**.

Simple print enables you to print a lower quality version of the image without the need to use **Adobe Acrobat Reader**. Select the image and click on the **Simple print** option. After printing, click on **Back to Resource Gallery**.

Slideshow presentation

If you would like to present a number of resources without having to return to the Resource Gallery and select a new image each time, you can compile a slideshow. Click on the **+** tabs at the top of each image in the Resource Gallery you would like to include in your presentation (pictures, sound and video can be included). It is important that you click on the images in the order in which you would like to view them (a number will appear on each tab to confirm the order). If you would like to change the order, click on **Clear slideshow** and begin again. Once you have selected your images – up to a maximum of 20 – click on **Play slideshow** and you will be presented with the first of your selected resources. To move to the next selection in your slideshow click on **Next slide**, to see a previous resource click on **Previous slide**. You can end your slideshow presentation at any time by clicking on **Resource Gallery**. Your slideshow selection will remain selected until you **Clear slideshow** or return to the **Menu screen**.

Viewing on an interactive whiteboard or data projector

Resources can be viewed directly from the CD. To make viewing easier for a whole class, use a large monitor, data projector or interactive whiteboard. For group, paired or individual work, the resources can be viewed from the computer screen.

Photocopiable resources (PDF format)

To view or print a photocopiable resource page, click on the required title in the list and the page will open as a read-only page in **Adobe Acrobat**. In order to access these files you will need to have already installed **Adobe Acrobat Reader** on your computer (see 'Setting up your computer for optimal use' above). To print the selected resource select **File** and then **Print**. Once you have printed the resource **minimise** or **close** the Adobe screen using — or **X** in the top right-hand corner of the screen. This will take you back to the list of PDF files. To return to the **Menu screen**, click on **Back**.

TOYS

Content, skills and concepts

This chapter links to unit 1 of the QCA Scheme of Work for history at Key Stage 1, 'How are our toys different from those in the past?', and so focuses on the theme of toys. Together with the Toys Resource Gallery on the CD-ROM, the chapter includes a range of sources, both visual and written, which can be used in teaching this unit. Like the QCA unit, the chapter looks at toys from the past and provides materials to support the teaching of similarities and differences between them and toys today. Oral history, discussion and the sorting and description of objects are all prior learning activities which will have introduced relevant skills and concepts to the children in the Foundation Stage, before they progress to learning the skills and concepts taught in this unit.

Resources on the CD-ROM

Pictures of toys from different times in the past are provided on the CD-ROM, some from Victorian and Edwardian times, others from the 1930s or post-war period and some that are relatively modern. Teacher's notes containing background information about these resources and suggesting ways to deliver teaching to the children, are provided in this chapter. Also on the CD-ROM is a film of an interview with a grandparent, talking about the toys she used to play with as a child. This will involve the children with real-life experiences from the past, in a format that is both accessible and engaging for the young child.

Photocopiable pages

Photocopiable resources can be found within the book and are also provided in PDF format on the CD-ROM, from which they can be printed. They include:
▶ word cards which highlight the essential vocabulary of this topic
▶ stories about toys
▶ writing frames.
The teacher's notes in this chapter which accompany the photocopiable resources include suggestions for ways of using the pages for whole class, group or individual activities. The activities suggested include cross-curricular links with literacy, art, design and technology, ICT and geography. There are also close links, wherever appropriate, with drama, in the form of ideas for structured play areas or small dramatic activities.

Stories

The stories on the photocopiable pages are designed to both interest the children in the pictures on the CD, and also to introduce them to notions of the past. They help enable children to make comparisons between the past and the present day. The stories have been written at different reading levels. This means they can be used for shared reading or for group work, as part of a guided reading session. Very able readers may be able to read one of the simpler stories themselves with support from an adult.

History skills

Skills such as observing, describing, sorting, sequencing, listening, speaking, reading, writing and drawing are involved in the activities provided in the teacher's notes for both the resources on the CD and in the book. For example, in thinking about old and modern dolls, the children will observe closely the differences between the two from comparing the pictures on the CD. They can learn to use descriptive vocabulary to describe and compare the two types of doll. They can listen to a story and perhaps be involved in sharing the reading of the story. They can then work on the suggested activities and complete the writing frame provided.

Historical understanding

In the course of the suggested tasks, a further overarching aim is for children to begin to develop their notions of old and new, the past and of the passing of time. They will begin to understand that things now are different in some ways from how they were in the past, but in other ways, the same. They will also begin to develop an awareness that there are different times in the past, and that these were also different from each other.

NOTES ON THE CD-ROM RESOURCES

Children with hoops

Boys and girls of all ages enjoyed playing with hoops like the ones shown in this picture since ancient times. It is thought that bowling hoops were popular in Medieval and Tudor times, when children began to play with the hoops taken from old water or wine barrels. In early Victorian times, the hoops would be made of metal or wood. Later on specially made wooden hoops were used. The hoop would be bowled along by hand or with a stick, with the child running alongside. Hoops remained popular toys right through Victorian times and into the 20th century, until the outbreak of war in 1939.

Discussing the picture

▶ Ask the children what they can see in the picture. Ask what the boy and girl are doing. Do any of them know what this toy is called?

▶ Ask the children how they think hoops were played with. Describe how they would have been bowled along the street. Do the children think it was easy to do?

▶ Ask if they have ever seen anyone playing with a hoop. Did they roll it along like this?

▶ Do they think the boy and girl are playing with their hoops now, or do they think this picture was made a long time ago? Ask what kind of picture the children think it is, for instance a photograph, or a painting.

▶ Discuss how the picture is an old one. Ask if there is anything about the boy and girl that tells us the picture is an old one. How do they know? Discuss the style of their clothes and explain how they are different from children's clothes today.

▶ Ask the children to compare the picture of the children with hoops with their own games at playtime.

Activities

▶ Show the children the picture of the 'Modern teddy' (provided on the CD). Ask the children which is the old picture and which is the new one. Ask for a volunteer to come to the front and put the two pictures in order, first the old one then the new one. Use the word cards (photocopiable page 20) to label the pictures *old* and *new*.

▶ Ask the children to list the different things they can see in the picture.

▶ In a PE lesson, provide enough hoops for the children to work in pairs. Give them the opportunity to practise bowling the hoops along the floor in turn. Finish with some small group races. Discuss with the children how easy it was to bowl the hoops.

▶ Ask why they think children don't play with hoops in the streets now (the streets are too busy and dangerous because of fast cars and lorries).

▶ Compare the picture with the 'K'nex car' (provided on the CD) or, alternatively, ask the children to bring to school a modern toy of their own. Ask them what is different about how they play with modern toys (old-fashioned toys like hoops were simple to play with; modern toys need more knowledge and different skills, especially construction-kit toys). What is different about how the toys work?

K'nex car

This very modern toy is constructed by the child themselves from a pack of ready prepared materials. It is fundamentally different from the simple hoops of Victorian children, requiring considerable knowledge of model construction on the part of the child. These toys are often bought by parents with an educational purpose in mind, since they develop children's motor skills and increase their dexterity. Unlike early toys, they represent the adult world to some extent and behave realistically when the children play with them.

Discussing the toy

▶ Discuss what kind of toy this is. Have the children seen one like this before?

▶ Ask how they know that it is meant to be a car. What parts are not really like a car? Ask if they know why this is.

▶ Ask if anyone in the class has ever made a K'nex toy or similar, or if someone has helped them to make one. Discuss whether it was difficult or not.

► Look at the parts used to make the car. Ask the children to count some of them, such as the wheels, the blue parts, and so on.
► Find out how many different car parts the children can name, such as *wheels*, *axle*.

Activities

► Discuss whether the children think this is a modern toy or an old one, and how they know. Make a list on the board of suggestions why the class think it is a modern toy, for example that it is made from plastic, that it is brightly coloured. Make another list of words that suggest why a toy, such as a Victorian hoop, is old. Compare the lists and draw out the changes in technology for the children, such as the use of plastic instead of natural materials like wood.
► Encourage the children to bring in examples of constructional toys they have at home. Allow them time to make some toys and then ask some of them to explain to the class how they did this.
► As part of a shared writing session, write some simple instructions on how to put together a toy car from a kit.
► Provide constructional toys for the children to use, ensuring that boys and girls have equal access to the toys. Display the models made and encourage the children to label their models with their names.
► Make up a class story about an adventure experienced by a toy car.

Clockwork aeroplane

Clockwork was an early type of mechanism used to animate toys, and these were produced throughout Victorian times and the 20th century. This clockwork aeroplane, from the 1930s, although replicating an advanced 20th-century technological development, uses a very early type of technology both in the form of energy used and the material used to make it.

Discussing the picture

► Ask the children what they can see in the picture. Is it a real aeroplane?
► Ask them what they think it is made from. Explain that it is a toy aeroplane made from wood. Write the word *wooden* on the board. This will introduce text in relation to the picture and encourage the children to read.
► Explain to the class that although the aeroplane in the picture is not a real aeroplane, it still worked. Can they think how children would have made it work? Discuss the fact that it is a clockwork plane. Show them a clock or clockwork toy and demonstrate how it has to be wound up by hand in order to work.
► Ask if they think this one actually flew in the air. Why might it not have done? (Too heavy, or not powerful enough.) Discuss how the plane might simply have rolled along the ground on its wheels, as planes do before they take off.
► Ask the children if they think this looks like a very modern aeroplane. If not, how do they know?

Activities

► Compare the aeroplane with the picture of the 'Children with hoops' (provided on the CD). Ask if they think the plane is newer than the toy hoops (it is newer). Discuss how this kind of toy came later on, after the time in the picture of the children with the hoops.
► Provide the children with a variety of clocks and wind-up toys, and allow time for them to play with them, discussing how they work as the children play. This could be a small group activity, or part of a structured play area in the classroom.

► Provide paper, crayons and pencils, or chalk and a board for the children to draw some clockwork toys.
► Compare the aeroplane with the 'Remote-controlled car' photograph (provided on the CD). The children could look at the materials the two toys are made from, and also at how they would play with them. The plane would be 'flown' by hand, while the car is self-powered.
► Play the interview 'Toys I used to play with' (provided on the CD). Look at the part where Sheila talks about winding up her train to play with it.

Remote-controlled car

In sharp contrast to the hoop, and even the clockwork toy, the remote-controlled car depends upon a high level of technology and modern energy sources to power it. A highly advanced form of animation, remote-controlled toys are popular with both children and adults. Higher levels of understanding and skill are required to operate such toys effectively, very different from the simple physical skills needed to play with earlier toys. Children need considerable understanding: a knowledge of how electrical power sources work; understanding of the technology used to operate the toy; directional awareness and fine motor skills to manipulate the controls in order to move the toy accurately along its intended path. Children need a new layer of technological understanding to play with modern toys like these. This remote-controlled car is assembled from a construction kit, and so requires a wide range of constructional skills along with those already mentioned.

Discussing the toy

▶ Ask the children what they think this toy is. Is it modern or old fashioned? How do they know? (It is brightly coloured, it looks as though it is made of plastic, and so on.)
▶ What do they think it can do? How do they think they could play with it?
▶ Ask if they have heard the words *remote-controlled* before. Do they know what this means?
▶ Ask if anyone has a remote-controlled toy at home. Can they explain how it moves?
▶ Ask if the children know of any other toys, or other things, that work by remote control in real life, for example traffic lights, train signals.
▶ Ask if they think there were remote-controlled cars a long time ago, for example when children played with hoops in the street. Ask why not.
▶ Do they think it's more fun to play with toys like this modern one? Do they think it is harder than playing with simple toys like hoops?

Activities

▶ Use a roamer, such as a floor turtle, to show how toys can be programmed to move in different directions. Make a road or pathway for the children to practise manipulating the roamer along.
▶ Talk about how the roamer works and how it moves in different directions. Compare this with the 'Clockwork aeroplane' picture (provided on the CD). Discuss what makes the roamer move and how this is different from the clockwork toys of the past.
▶ If possible, bring in a remote-controlled toy and show how it works, allowing the children to play with it, or invite the children to bring in their own remote-controlled toys, if appropriate.
▶ Look at the 'Children with hoops' and 'Clockwork aeroplane' pictures (provided on the CD). Discuss how the remote-controlled car is the most modern of the three toys.
▶ Use some of the word cards (photocopiable pages 20–1) and ask the children to attribute words they think are appropriate to the picture of the car, such as *shiny*, *modern*.

Lead soldiers

Lead soldiers, both on foot and on horseback, like these Victorian Irish Lancers, have been popular for many years, and both collecting and playing with such soldiers remains a hobby for people even today. These Irish Lancers were probably made some time after 1893, when a process was invented for casting hollow toy soldiers from lead. Models such as these illustrate in detail the uniform, headgear and weaponry used by specific types of soldier, and as such, they are very realistic images of warfare in a bygone age. In addition to this, however, they provide children with the raw material for flights of imagination into fantasy encounters with the enemy, or, as was frequent in the past, re-enactments of famous battles and victories. Originally, they would have been bought or collected in their dozens in order to make up complete battalions of either side in a battle, so that the battle could then by replayed in minute detail. Since they are made of lead, however, care needs to be taken if real examples are to be handled by young children.

Discussing the picture

▶ Ask the children what they can see in the picture.
▶ Why do they think these men are dressed in this way? Explain, if the children do not know, that they are soldiers dressed in their special uniforms.

▶ Ask the children to say what the soldiers are wearing, for example helmets, red and blue tunics, striped trousers, boots. Discuss how these toys show us what soldiers really looked like in the past. Ask if the children think soldiers look like this now.

▶ Ask what they think the soldiers have in their hands. The children may think these are spears. Explain that they were like spears, but were called *lances*, and so the soldiers were called *lancers*. Their job was to charge at the enemy and try to knock them off their horses, or to knock them down.

▶ Ask if the children know what we call soldiers who ride on horses (cavalry). Explain about the use of cavalry and why horses were used in battle in the past (to make the first charge and to confuse the enemy).

▶ Ask if the class can suggest how children long ago would have played with these soldiers. (They would have arranged them in battle order, ranging them against a set of 'enemy' soldiers, moving them around on a large table or on the nursery floor.)

Activities

▶ If possible, provide some examples of old lead soldiers for the children to see. Explain to the children that we now know that lead is dangerous for children to handle, so they will be able to look closely at the soldiers but won't be able to touch them. Focus on the colours of the uniforms and the weapons the toys have.

▶ Provide some model soldiers from the present. Ask the class if they are made from the same materials. Discuss how the old soldiers are made from metal, and ask the children what the new ones are made from.

▶ Compare this picture with the picture of 'Action Man' (provided on the CD). Can they tell you which picture shows an old toy and which a modern one? Make a note of the children who appear to understand this difference, for your assessment records.

▶ Use 'Old and new toys' on photocopiable page 26 for the children to record information about the age of the lead soldiers in comparison to Action Man.

Action Man

In contrast to the lead soldiers of the past, this modern 'action man' is a highly imaginative robotic image. Although there are more conventional modern soldier versions of Action Man, this futuristic model, and other toys of this kind, is drawn from heroic fictional TV or film characters. Totally different in its conceptualisation from the lead soldiers, Action Man still enables children to imagine and engage in battles and enemy encounters. The weapons and armour used by this Action Man reflect the space age, and somewhat fictional culture, in which modern children live. While Action Man and lead soldiers cannot be more different in their appearance and origins, both are tools that stimulate children's minds to invent battles and adventures in faraway places, and as such, they can be seen to serve exactly the same needs.

Discussing the picture

▶ Ask the children what they can see in the picture. Do they recognise or like this kind of toy? Why do they?

▶ Ask if they think this toy is old fashioned or new. How do they know? Draw the children's attention to the style of Action Man, the kind of materials he is made from, his weapons and so on.

▶ Ask the children to think of words to describe Action Man, for example *fierce, strong, pretend, from the future*, and so on. Write some of their suggestions on the board.

▶ Ask the children if they think there are real people who do the things that the Action Man in the picture does. Explain how he, and other characters like him, are made up and only do things in stories. Ask the class to list all the super-human heroes that they have heard of, such as Batman, Superwoman, Robocop.

Activities

▶ Provide an Action Man, or a similar kind of modern toy, for the children to look at.

▶ Compare this picture with the picture of the 'Lead soldiers' (provided on the CD). Write on the board *old* and *new* to model the writing and spelling of the words, and ask the children to read them. Ask for volunteers to find these words from amongst the word cards (on photocopiable page 20), and then to place the correct word card by the picture of each toy.

▶ Use the writing frame 'Old and new toys' on photocopiable page 26 for the children to record information about the age of Action Man in comparison to the lead soldiers.

▶ Invite any children who have toys like Action Man to bring them into school. Allow time for the children to show their toys and to describe how they play with them to the class.

▶ If possible, look at video games or computer games which feature imaginary characters.

▶ Allow time for the children to draw pictures of Action Man or other heroic characters and make a wall display of their work.

China-faced doll

Dolls have been made throughout the ages, for a variety of purposes, by most cultures around the world. Generally, very early dolls were made of wood or bone. From around the 4th century, wax became a popular medium, initially for making commemorative dolls or masks at funerals. In the 18th century, fashion dolls began to be produced in France to publicise new fashions in costume and hairstyles. Soon wax workers were commissioned to make play dolls to meet a rising demand. At the end of the 19th century, the secret of how to use kaolin to harden porcelain or china clay was discovered. This secret was guarded carefully in Germany for many years and china dolls' heads were exported all over the world from factories in Meissen. The dolls' heads were all very much the same, however, and so the dolls they were used for tended to be dressed in local regional styles in order to differentiate them. Because of the fragility of these dolls' heads, the industry grew rapidly and great profits were made until new unbreakable materials were invented for doll making. The doll in this picture is Victorian.

Discussing the picture

▶ Ask the children what they can see in the picture. Do they think it is a modern doll, or an old-fashioned one? Write the words *old* and *modern* on the board. This will model the writing process to the children and present an opportunity to discuss how the words are opposites.

▶ Ask them why they think this, for instance her clothes look different from clothes we wear today. Explain any features they do not understand from the picture, such as the face is made from porcelain, or china clay, and it could break very easily.

▶ Look at the clothes the doll is wearing. Ask the children for words to describe them.

▶ Ask the children if they have seen any dolls like this. If so, where have they seen them?

▶ Explain that these dolls are very, very old and are also very expensive, because there are not many left now. Explain how children would have had to be very careful when they played with dolls like this one, because they could break so easily.

Activities

▶ Read 'The story of the china-faced doll' (photocopiable page 23) with the class to reinforce the concept of this doll being old and fragile.

▶ Compare this picture with that of 'Sindy' (provided on the CD). What can the children say is the same about the two dolls? What do they think is different?

▶ Make a collection of dolls for the toy corner or in a created toy shop, and allow time for the children to play with them.

▶ Organise sorting activities with a collection of dolls, according to size, costume, colours or age.

▶ Ask the children to draw pictures of the dolls and label them using the word cards on photocopiable pages 20–1.

▶ Make a class book of dolls using the children's drawings and labels.

▶ See if the children, working individually or in pairs, can place a collection of dolls according to whether they are older or newer. Make a note of the children who can do this unaided for your assessment records.

Sindy

A very popular modern doll, Sindy is often seen dressed in the type of clothes typical of the modern young person. Children can change her outfit as they wish, from casual to very formal, beachwear to evening wear. Here she is dressed in a ballerina's costume, in the role of a fairy. Often made to epitomise the ultimate in glamour, Sindy, and similar dolls have been heavily criticised for presenting females as a set of stereotypical images, and for attempting to inculcate children into the worst excesses of consumerism. Nevertheless, they have brought genuine

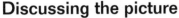

pleasure to the countless little girls who have enjoyed the opportunity to fantasise as they dress them in their different outfits and play with them in different roles.

Discussing the picture

▶ Ask if anyone knows the name of this doll. Ask if any of the children have one at home, or if any other children they live with have one.
▶ Discuss Sindy's appearance. What is she wearing? What does she have on her feet? Why does she have wings?
▶ What sort of character do the children think Sindy might be (a fairy, a ballerina).
▶ Ask which children might like to play with a doll like this. Why?
▶ What sort of games might the children play with her?
▶ Ask if there is anyone in the class who does not like Sindy. Ask why this is.

Activities

▶ Discuss with the class whether Sindy is a new or an old doll. How do they know?
▶ Provide drawing materials for the children to draw Sindy. Suggest they make up a glamorous doll character of their own to draw. Make a display of the children's work and encourage them to choose names for their dolls and to make labels for their pictures.
▶ Find stories about dolls and fairies, such as Tinkerbell in JM Barrie's *Peter Pan*, to share with the class. In shared writing time, make up some stories with the children about fairies.
▶ Talk about how in the past, many people believed in fairies. Make a list of all the imaginary creatures that have existed in history, such as ghosts, goblins, witches, giants, dwarves. Make a collection of books containing stories about these fictitious characters to use during shared reading or story time.
▶ Collect some old long dresses, ballet shoes, and so on, and make a dressing-up corner for the children to use as a structured play area. Other clothes suitable for witches and wizards could also be added to the collection.

Edwardian teddy

Brown bears, the image on which the original teddy bear was based, were traditional toys in Russia for many centuries. Mishka the bear is a common feature in many Russian folk tales. However, the first teddy bears appeared around 1903 when the new toy, designed primarily as a boy's doll, was created. The idea arose from a meeting between an American toy dealer and a German toy maker, Margarette Steiff. The notion arose in the mind of the American from an illustration of the then President, Theodore (Teddy) Roosevelt, taken after a bear hunt in the Rocky Mountains. At Roosevelt's feet was a small bear that he had refused to shoot. The toy dealer suggested that a bear's head should replace that of the doll, and the body of the doll be covered in a brown plush material to resemble the bear's fur. The name *teddy bear* was based on that of Teddy Roosevelt. Within a few years there were hundreds of factory and home workers employed in making these early teddy bears. The bears were fairly lifelike, however, with long front legs to enable them to stand on all fours. They had small eyes and ears and fairly lifelike faces. The Edwardian teddies in this picture are typical of these bears.

1930s teddy

This teddy bear dates from the 1930s. Teddies at this time were made to be strong and to last. They were filled with tough materials, such as horsehair. This made them very stiff and firm to touch, however, unlike the cuddly bears produced today. They resembled the earlier Steiff bears in some ways, with their long arms, small ears and long snouts. Their eyes are smaller than those on modern bears, sometimes making them look fairly lifelike and fierce. They were covered in a plush material, which resembled as closely as possible the real fur of brown bears. By this time, however, they were becoming more friendly to look at with slightly more appealing expressions than the first, rather angry-looking bears that were made at the beginning of the 20th century.

Modern teddy

Barnaby Bear is a very modern teddy bear. The teddy has a distinct character and identity, having been made with a specific purpose in mind. Barnaby is an example of how the general idea of a bear has now diversified, so that it is possible to buy many different types of bear, such as baby bears, Pooh bears and so on. As you can see in the picture, Barnaby is a rather fictitious creature, with short, unusable legs, a flat face with no real bear-like snout, and an unrealistically fluffy coat. This bear is made to look friendly and cuddly, rather than the original purpose which was to resemble a real bear. Barnaby is a new, imaginary creation and in this sense, is rather like the Action Man (see the notes on page 11).

Discussing the pictures

▶ These three pictures of teddies could be used separately or as a group. If used as a group, ask the children to compare them and say what they think is different.
▶ Discuss the differences between the teddies with the children and the different ways in which the teddies were made. Explain how the oldest bears felt hard to the touch and how they looked more like real brown bears, with fierce expressions and long snouts.
▶ Ask which picture is most like the children's own teddies at home. Are theirs old-fashioned bears or more modern ones?
▶ Ask the children to name famous bears they have heard of, such as Rupert, Pooh, Paddington.

Activities

▶ Challenge the class to place the pictures of the teddies in chronological order. See if they can explain why they think one is the oldest, another the newest, and so on.
▶ Read some stories about famous teddies to the class, and show pictures of them. Discuss whether they are old or modern teddies.
▶ If possible, make a collection of as many different types of teddies as possible and allow the children time to play with and sort the bears.
▶ Look at the bear in the interview 'Toys I used to play with' (provided on the CD) and discuss with the children where this teddy might fit into a chronological sequence. Is he an old, or a new bear?
▶ Collect toy catalogues and ask the children to cut out as many pictures of teddies as they can and to sort them into old and modern teddies. Use the pictures for a wall display afterwards.
▶ Teach the children songs and rhymes about bears, such as 'Bear hunt' or 'Teddy bears' picnic'.
▶ Read the story of 'Bruin, the old teddy bear' on page 22.
▶ Give out copies of the word cards (on photocopiable pages 19–21) and ask the children to label each of the pictures.

Interview: Toys I used to play with

This interview, where Sheila Hogbin talks about the toys she remembers playing with as a child back in the 1930s, helps to ground this topic of toys in reality. Seeing Sheila talking shows children how older people, like their grandparents, played with toys, just as they do. It also shows that their grandparents' toys were often very much the same as modern ones. Sheila's teddy bear is an example of this and can be compared with the pictures of teddies on the CD. The bear is also an example of a toy that has been well-used, since Sheila was only one year old when she was given him. Sheila's comparisons of toys she played with and the toys children play with today are very helpful. She points out that children seem to have more toys to play with today, and how many of them are made of plastic. However, she also points out that many children's favourite toys today are still the same as in the past.

Discussing the interview

▶ Ask the children what the first toy was that Sheila had and how old she was. Why does Sheila feel he was so special to her?
▶ Ask the children if they can recall the toys Sheila mentions. What were her favourite toys?
▶ Can the class remember how old Sheila was when she got her train set? Who gave her the train? Why?

▶ What sort of toys does Sheila say girls usually had?
▶ Ask the children if they can remember which is the only toy Sheila says she still has left now.
▶ Ask the children which toys Sheila thinks have stayed the same, and which she says are new and different since she was a child.
▶ Ask what newly invented toys Sheila would have liked to play with when she was a child if she could have had them.

Activities
▶ Arrange for the children to bring to school their favourite toys. They can talk about them, just as Sheila did, draw and write about them, and complete the writing frame 'My very best toy' on photocopiable page 30.
▶ During a shared writing session, talk about how Sheila was answering questions. Work with groups of children or the whole class to write some more questions that they might ask Sheila.
▶ Organise the children into pairs, one working as the interviewer and one as the interviewee. Give the children time to practise this as a role-play activity, based on the interview they have seen.
▶ Devise other topics that the children would like to talk about and allow time for the children to talk about their interests in pairs, groups or as a whole class.

NOTES ON THE PHOTOCOPIABLE PAGES

Word cards   PAGES 19–21

Two specific types of vocabulary have been introduced on the word cards:
▶ words related to the passing of time and chronology, such as *before*, *after*, *modern* and *old*
▶ descriptive vocabulary to help the children learn to describe what they see, such as *shiny*, *clean*, *rusty* and *faded*.
Encourage the children to think of other appropriate words to add to these in order to build up a word bank with which to discuss the theme of toys. They could also use the cards in displays and to help them in writing captions for their pictures.

Activities
▶ Make copies of the word cards, cut them out and laminate them. Use them as often as possible when talking about toys.
▶ Encourage the children to match the words to pictures on the CD as often as possible. Provide pictures of groups of toys from the CD, such as the 'Lead soldiers', '1930s teddy' and the 'China-faced doll' and ask the children to choose word cards that describe the features common to the group, in this instance *old*, *long ago*, *then*.
▶ Read the word cards together during whole class plenaries. Follow this up with pairs of children reading the words. Check which words each child can read.
▶ Add the words to the class word bank, and encourage the children to write them frequently, for example adding them to their own pictures, or when using the writing/drawing frames in this book.

Stories about toys
These stories are intended to be shared with the children in ways appropriate to your class. They may be read to the class in story time, or used in the shared reading time within the Literacy Hour.
    The stories might be used as a stimulus for shared writing about another kind of toy in the classroom or one which has been brought in by a child. Pictures on the CD relate to the stories and can be used to illustrate them. Possibly, more able children could be encouraged to make up stories about a toy of their own to tell the class. They could form the beginning of a class collection of stories about toys, which you might put together from suggestions from the children and their parents or carers.

Bruin, the old teddy bear

This story is intended to link with the picture on the CD of the 'Edwardian teddy' and/or the '1930s teddy', and with other related work on teddy bears. The extract about the teddy bear from the interview 'Toys I used to play with' could also be used in relation to it. The teddy in the story has an old-fashioned name, since he is a bear from the relatively distant past. The story aims to introduce to young children the idea that a toy can be quite old because it belonged to a person who has now grown up. Other stories about teddies are, of course, numerous, such as Paddington, Pooh and Rupert, all stories which can enliven the topic for the very young child.

Discussing the story
▶ Ask the children what kind of toy this story is about.
▶ Ask if his name sounds unusual. Have they heard of this name before? Explain how it was a popular name for teddies a long time ago. What names do their teddies have?
▶ Ask the class if they can think why Bruin should be unhappy. Ask what Bruin did not like.
▶ Ask them why they think the sounds and voices were familiar to Bruin.
▶ Can the children remember from the story who Bruin used to belong to a long time ago, when he was a new teddy?
▶ What do the children think *elated* means?
▶ Why do the children think that the little boy must take special care of Bruin?

Activities
▶ Arrange with the children's parents or carers for them to bring in their own old teddies one day. Ask the children to bring in their own new teddies. Look carefully at the teddies and compare them. Ask the children what they think the differences are between them.
▶ Organise time for the children to draw pictures of their teddies.
▶ Make the children's pictures into a class book of teddies. Help the children to write the names of their teddies below their pictures.
▶ During circle time put out a collection of teddies and challenge the children to sort the teddies in as many ways as they can, such as tallest to shortest or oldest to newest.
▶ Write a class story about old and new bears.

The story of the china-faced doll

This story provides young children with some awareness of how dolls were made differently in the past, and from different materials. It also shows how difficult it used to be when playing with dolls like these, because of their fragility and the delicate nature of the clothes these dolls would have been dressed in. Discussion could, therefore, move on to cover what it was like to play with toys in the past.

Discussing the story
▶ Ask the children what kind of toy Suzannah is.
▶ Where was Suzannah at the beginning of the story?
▶ Why do the children think that Granny was more interested in Suzannah than Jane was?
▶ What happened to Suzannah when she got back to Jane's house?
▶ What did Jane have to be careful about? Ask the children why they think she has to be careful with Suzannah.

Activities
▶ Arrange for the children to bring in their dolls and other toys. Make a toyshop for the children to use as a structured play area.
▶ During shared writing time, make up some sentences about a doll in a toyshop.
▶ Use the writing frame 'Drawing the china-faced doll' on photocopiable page 27 to extend the children's understanding of chronology, using this story.
▶ Make a simple folding book with three pages for each child. Provide drawing materials for the children to draw a sequence of three pictures, in which the china-faced doll has a small adventure.
▶ Provide materials for the children to make some model dolls of their own, such as a rag or a peg doll.

The Dumb Soldier

PAGE 24

This poem was first published in Robert Louis Stevenson's collection of poems *A Child's Garden of Verses* in 1885. The poems were all based on Stevenson's own childhood memories and clearly portray fantasies, feelings and pastimes from a child's perception. This poem is quite a challenging one for young children to understand – the vocabulary is difficult in places and they may find the verse difficult to follow. Words like *dumb*, *apace*, *scythe*, *grenadier* will need to be explained. The poem is best read to the children, and then discussed and explained to them in some detail if necessary. You may feel that perhaps just the first five verses are sufficient for your class, since these could be used separately from the other verses. More able children might well be able to understand the remaining verses, however, which describe the toy soldier's experiences.

Discussing the poem
▶ Read the title and the name of the poet to the class. Ask if they have heard of this poet before. Explain that he is well known for his poems, especially those he wrote for children.
▶ Talk about the title of the poem, especially the meaning of the word *dumb*.
▶ Give the children a copy of the poem and read it, or perhaps just the first five verses, to them. Ask if anyone can say where the toy soldier is and why he cannot be found.
▶ Ask why he looks up with *leaden eyes*. What is a *scythe* and why is it *stoned*? What does the poet mean when he says the lawn is *shaven clear*?
▶ What do the class think the child in the poem is going to do when the lawn is mown short?

Activities
▶ Ask the class to look at the clues that tell us it is an old poem. Record the children's suggestions, such as the date, the old-fashioned words.
▶ Show the children the picture of the 'Lead soldiers' (provided on the CD). Ask the children if the soldiers are like the one in the poem.
▶ During PE, suggest that the children demonstrate how soldiers long ago would have marched. Use some military marching music for the children to practise their steps to and help them imagine that they are like the soldier in the poem.
▶ Ask the class to think of other toys that might get lost. Discuss what places they may be lost in, and then write some sentences together about toys being lost and then found again.

The lead soldier

PAGE 25

This story can be used alongside the picture of the 'Lead soldiers' on the CD, or to provide contextual detail to accompany the use of some real examples of these toys. It aims to introduce children to some descriptive vocabulary to describe toy soldiers, and in particular, cavalrymen, and also to an initial awareness of the important role of the cavalry in warfare at the time of the Crimean War. The cavalry was often used to make the first charge against the enemy so that it would then be easier for the foot soldiers to make their assault. They would also sometimes gallop into a battle from the sides, causing confusion and panic amongst the enemy. The size and speed of the horses were used to try to frighten the enemy. The lead soldier in the story acts out in the nursery some of the famous victories won by the British army in the 19th century, such as the Battle of Sebastopol during the Crimean War. Like the soldier in the Robert Louis Stevenson poem, 'The Dumb Soldier' (photocopiable page 24), this toy soldier has had many experiences that he can remember. This story might be used together with the poem during work on literacy, to compare poetry and prose.

Discussing the story
▶ Ask the children what kind of toy this story is about.
▶ Ask the children if they know what the word *proud* means. Why was the lead soldier so proud? Ask how the lead soldier knew he was an important toy.
▶ Ask if anyone can explain where the lead soldier used to play. What was the nursery?
▶ Look at some of the special words in the story, like *uniform*, *lance*, *helmet*, *plume*, *tack*, *battles*, *cavalry*. Discuss and explain what they mean with the class.
▶ Explain how Britain was involved in many wars and battles in the nineteenth century, and how the cavalry was very important.
▶ Ask if the children think the lancer in the story would look smart.

Activities

▶ Provide art materials for the children to make their own pictures of lead soldiers.

▶ Working with the whole class, compose a short adventure story about a soldier in a war.

▶ Make a collection of modern soldiers and display these alongside the picture of the 'Lead soldiers' on the CD. Discuss the differences between them, and focus on how the equipment of modern soldiers has changed. Discuss why this has happened.

Writing/drawing frames

These photocopiable pages have been designed to become gradually more difficult. Children at this stage may only just be in the earliest stages of learning to read and write words, therefore, the activities suggested focus initially on drawing and the writing of simple words or captions. The tasks gradually incorporate sequencing more pictures and writing more words. More challenging vocabulary related to the concept of time and chronology is also gradually introduced. The final writing frame (photocopiable page 30) is open-ended for children to choose a toy of their own that they might want to draw and write about, and is designed to challenge more advanced writers.

Some of the writing frames require the children to draw or write about pictures from the CD, such as the 'Action Man' or the 'Clockwork aeroplane'. In these instances you may wish to print out copies of the pictures to give to the children to help with their drawing and writing.

Old and new toys

PAGE 26

This sheet introduces children to the very simplest of ideas related to chronology, the notion of *old* and *new*. Very obvious examples have been suggested, in the form of the 'Lead soldiers' and the 'Action Man' (provided on the CD), and it is recommended that discussion and explanation take place before the children attempt this kind of activity themselves.

Drawing the china-faced doll

PAGE 27

This writing and drawing frame also focuses on developing an initial awareness of chronology. It introduces children to ordering pictures in a simple sequence and to the associated vocabulary of *before* and *after*. It could be used in conjunction with other examples which use the same vocabulary of ordering, such as aspects of the children's daily routine, for example *I get up before I eat my breakfast*, *I go to school after I have eaten my breakfast*.

Order the toys

PAGE 28

This frame extends the notion of ordering a little further, so that the children need to sort three pictures into the correct sequence. It also develops further their use of related vocabulary, such as *newer* and *newest*. Again, a wide range of other pictures could be used in a similar way, or children could be asked, perhaps as an assessment task, to draw their own examples in a sequence of three.

Oldest and newest toys

PAGE 29

This sheet requires children to focus more directly on writing activities. It makes further use of the superlatives *oldest* and *newest*, and again needs to be used following discussion and explanation of the meaning and correct use of these words. It would be useful to work through some similar examples to model the process of sentence-completion with the children.

My very best toy

PAGE 30

This writing and drawing frame enables children to decide on their own picture to draw and then provides an open-ended writing task for them to complete. The level of support provided in completing this frame will depend on the needs of individual children. The most able writers will be able to write their own description of their favourite toy. The activity would be most effective if it could be carried out when children have brought their favourite toys into school, so that they can write about them while looking at them. Alternatively, it may make a good homework sheet.

Time word cards

before
after
now
then
when they were young
long ago

modern

old

new

worn out

broken

Old and new word cards (2)

dirty	**rusty**
faded	**shiny**
clean	**colourful**

Bruin, the old teddy bear

Bruin was feeling very sad. He did not know why this was. He lived in a pretty house, and although he was getting very old, he was always warm and comfortable on the shelf in the toy cupboard. Each day was quiet and peaceful. He was only disturbed occasionally when Mrs Pimm, the cleaner, dusted his shelf.

He did remember one terrible day, when Mrs Pimm had said he was getting too dusty. She lifted him up and used a horrible noisy machine with a long pipe to suck all the dust away. It was very annoying for Bruin, especially when his nose and ears were sucked up into the pipe!

Apart from that, Bruin could not remember very much. The days were all the same and toy bears do not have very good memories. Why was he so sad, he wondered?

Then, one day, Bruin heard a familiar sound. It was children's voices and feet running up and down the stairs. Light poured in as the door of the toy cupboard opened. Suddenly, Bruin was being lifted off his shelf by familiar hands.

"He's still here!" exclaimed the voice he knew so well. Now Bruin could see the face too – it was his old childhood playmate, William, who looked different somehow. "Maybe he is older too, like me," thought Bruin.

William handed Bruin to a little boy, who looked very like him.

"Here's my old favourite teddy bear. He was my grandfather's teddy, a long time ago. He's yours to play with now. Make sure you look after him well, as I did," said William.

Bruin was elated. At last he remembered happier days and now they would begin all over again. Bruin was a happy teddy bear again at last.

SCHOLASTIC PHOTOCOPIABLE

The story of the china-faced doll

Suzannah was a china-faced doll. She lived in a big old junk shop, where there were lots of different toys and other things for sale. Suzannah lived with lots of other dolls, but she did not like what they said to her. They would say, "You don't speak like us. You use very old-fashioned words, and what a strange name you have. You think you are better than we are, but you are not. You are just an old junk doll like us."

Suzannah really did not know why her words came out sounding different from all the other dolls. She knew she had been in the shop much longer than the others, but she did not know why she was different.

One rainy day, an old lady came into the shop with a little girl. They had come in to shelter from the rain. They looked around for a while, then the little girl spotted the dolls. "Oh look, Granny, look at all these. Can I have one?"

Granny came across and they both began to search for a doll that they liked. All at once, Granny exclaimed, "Jane, look at that one there. It's just like one I had when I was a girl."

Granny was looking at Suzannah. But Jane did not like Suzannah. "She's all dirty and horrible," she said, but Granny replied, "I think if we take her home and give her a wash, you will have a big surprise. Shall we try?"

"Oh alright," said Jane. "We'll take her and see."

Back at the house, Granny and Jane carefully washed Suzannah's face. They had to be very, very careful, because she was an old doll. They washed her dress and cleaned her shoes very carefully too. These things were very delicate and Granny knew that they would tear or break if they were not treated very gently. When they had finished Jane was delighted, and so was Granny. "She looks really good now, doesn't she," said Jane, "but I still think she looks a bit odd."

"Yes," said Granny, "that's because she is a very old doll with a china clay face. I'm glad we found her, because she really is quite old." Soon, Jane got so used to the old doll, that she loved her just as much as all her other dolls, although she had to keep her safe from the usual games she played with her toys.

The Dumb Soldier

When the grass was closely mown,
Walking on the lawn alone,
In the turf a hole I found
And hid a soldier underground.

Spring and daisies came apace;
Grasses hide my hiding-place;
Grasses run like a green sea
O'er the lawn up to my knee.

Under grass alone he lies,
Looking up with leaden eyes,
Scarlet coat and pointed gun,
To the stars and to the sun.

When the grass is ripe like grain,
When the scythe is stoned again,
When the lawn is shaven clear,
Then my hole shall reappear.

I shall find him, never fear,
I shall find my grenadier;
But for all that's gone and come,
I shall find my soldier dumb.

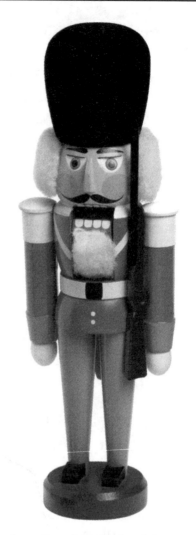

He has lived, a little thing,
In the grassy woods of spring;
Done, if he could tell me true,
Just as I should like to do.

He has seen the starry hours
And the springing of the flowers;
And the fairy things that pass
In the forests of the grass.

In the silence he has heard
Talking bee and ladybird,
And the butterfly has flown
O'er him as he lay alone.

Not a word will he disclose,
Not a word of all he knows.
I must lay him on the shelf,
And make up the tale myself.

by Robert Louis Stevenson (1850-1894)

The lead soldier

One sunny day in 1895 a little Victorian lead soldier woke up and yawned. It was difficult to stretch as he was packed snugly together with a jumble of other soldiers in a little wooden box. As he yawned he wondered what exciting adventures he might encounter that day.

The lead soldier was a very proud toy. He knew that he was very important, because the children in the house took him out to play every day. He had a wonderful red and blue uniform, with gold braid and decorations. Not only this, but he held a long, sharp lance, for fighting enemies. He had brightly polished boots and a smart helmet with a plume on top, making him look even taller and more important. The thing that the lead soldier was most proud of, however, was his wonderful black horse, with its shining mane and polished tack.

The lead soldier remembered the many battles he had taken part in on the nursery table. Racing ahead as part of the cavalry charge, the lead soldier knew he had helped to win many famous victories. He knew that many of the toy battles he had won were just like the real ones that real soldiers had fought, like the Battle of Sebastopol in the famous Crimean War. The lead soldier was very proud to be a cavalryman.

© Photodisc via SODA

Old and new toys

△ Draw a lead soldier and Action Man in the boxes to match the sentences. Write *old* and *new* below each picture.

Here is an old <u>lead soldier toy</u>.

Action Man is a <u>new</u> toy.

new

old

Drawing the china-faced doll

△ Draw the china-faced doll when she was in the junk shop. Then draw her in her new home. Read the words in the boxes. Write *before* and *after* below each picture.

This is the china-faced doll _before_ Granny and Jane found her.

This is the china-faced doll _after_ Granny and Jane found her.

before

after

Order the toys

△ Draw pictures of the children with hoops, the clockwork aeroplane and the remote-controlled car.

[ ] [ ] [ ]

△ Put the toys in order from the oldest to the newest. Then copy the right words below each box.

old   **newer**   **newest**

Oldest and newest toys

This is a picture of
the toy I would like
to play with.

I looked at pictures of _____

I thought the oldest toy was _____

because _____

I thought the newest toy was _____

because _____

My very best toy

My very best toy is my _____

Here is a picture of my very best toy.

I like to play with my very best toy because _____

_____

HOMES

Content, skills and concepts

This chapter links to unit 2 of the QCA Scheme of Work for history at Key Stage 1, 'What were homes like a long time ago?', and so focuses on the theme of homes. It aims to assist in planning, resourcing and meeting the objectives set for this unit. Together with the Homes Resource Gallery on the CD-ROM the chapter includes a range of sources, both visual and written, which can be used in teaching this unit. Like the QCA unit, the chapter looks at different types of homes, at homes from the past and household objects. It provides materials to support the teaching of similarities and differences between homes today and homes in the past. Oral history, discussion and the sorting and description of objects are all prior learning activities which will have introduced relevant skills and concepts to the children in the Foundation Stage, before they progress to the skills and concepts in this unit.

Resources on the CD-ROM

Pictures of homes, domestic scenes and domestic objects from different times in the past are provided on the CD-ROM, some from Victorian or Edwardian times, others from the 1930s or Second World War period and some which are modern. Teacher's notes containing background information about these resources, discussion points and activities for the classroom are provided in this chapter.

Photocopiable pages

Photocopiable resources can be found within the book and are also provided in PDF format on the CD-ROM, from which they can be printed. They include:
▶ word cards, which highlight the essential vocabulary of this topic
▶ a timeline
▶ stories about homes
▶ writing/drawing frames.

Teacher's notes are provided in this chapter to accompany these photocopiable text resources. These include suggestions for ways of using the pages as whole-class, or as group or individual activities.

Stories

The stories on the photocopiable pages are designed to both interest the children in the pictures on the CD, and also to introduce them to notions of the past. They aim to enable children to make comparisons between the past and the present day. The stories have been written at different reading levels. This will enable teachers to use them for shared reading or to share them with a group, as part of a guided reading session. Very able readers may be able to read one of the simpler stories themselves, with support from an adult.

History skills

Skills such as observing, describing, sorting, sequencing, comparing, inferring, listening, speaking, reading, writing and drawing are involved in the activities provided in the teacher's notes for both the resources on the CD and in the book. For example, in thinking about old-fashioned and modern homes, the children will observe closely the differences between the two by comparing the pictures on the CD. They can learn to use descriptive vocabulary to describe and compare the two types of home. They can be involved in sharing the reading of a story and then complete the writing frames provided.

Historical understanding

In the course of the suggested tasks, a further overarching aim is for children to begin to develop their notions of old and new, the past and of the passing of time. They will begin to understand that things now are different in some ways from how they were in the past, but in other ways, the same. They will also begin to develop an awareness that there are different times in the past, and that these were also different from each other.

NOTES ON THE CD-ROM RESOURCES

Victorian house

This Victorian terraced house was built in 1896, as part of a long row of houses, probably to provide fairly cheap and economical housing. Many terraces of this kind are still in use today and can be seen in many urban areas across the UK. They were built in an age of coal fires, and so each house has its own chimney and tall chimney pots. Very often, houses of this kind were roofed with slate, but this one appears to have been re-roofed with modern tiles. The sash windows remain much as they were when the house was first built, each section made up of several panes of glass. The doorway is sheltered by a small, arched porch and extra light is admitted into the hall through a pane of glass set above the doorframe. A characteristic feature of older urban houses is the metal railing enclosing the front garden.

Modern house

This is a photograph of a modern, newly built detached house. It has many significant differences when compared with houses built in Victorian or Edwardian times. New features include the garage and driveway, reflecting modern transport needs. There is a television aerial, which shows one of the key technological developments of the 20th century. There is a larger front garden than in many older homes, and there are blinds at the windows rather than curtains. While there are some rather old-fashioned features, such as gabled roofs and windows with several panes, these features reflect the demand for nostalgia in modern house building, which has resulted in a curious mixture of styles. Features characteristic of Victorian buildings are, therefore, beginning to reappear in modern ones.

Discussing the photographs

▶ Ask the children what is different about each house, for example there are more windows in the modern house and they are made from larger panes of glass; the modern house has no chimney.

▶ Discuss the features of each house, introducing appropriate vocabulary to describe them. (Make use of the word cards on photocopiable pages 43–7 if appropriate.)

▶ Discuss the materials from which each type of house is made. Are there different materials used to build the modern home, compared with the older one? (The roofs of old houses would usually be slate, as in the roof over the bay window in the picture; in new houses, they are usually tiled. Old houses had wooden window frames; modern ones PVC.)

▶ Ask the children why some things have changed in modern housing, such as why there is no chimney, why there is a garage and a TV aerial.

▶ Discuss the many different kinds of homes the children know of. Talk about why people live in such a variety of homes.

Activities

▶ Ask the children to place both of the pictures on the class timeline (see also photocopiable page 50).

▶ Using magazines, newspapers and catalogues, make a collection of pictures showing different types of homes. Get the children to work in pairs to sort the homes into different categories. Talk about the different kinds they might find, such as detached houses, semi-detached houses, bungalows, caravans, and so on.

▶ Give groups of children pictures of different homes and appropriate word cards (photocopiable pages 43–5). Ask the children to match the words to the correct homes. Discuss whether the children think the homes are old or modern as they carry out this task, to assess their understanding of *old* and *new*.

▶ Organise a walk around the locality. Look at the different types of homes and discuss the names for these with the class. Look at the features of the different buildings and encourage the children to look at the materials the homes are made from. Take pictures of the homes using a digital camera and add them to the collection you have made.

▶ Ask the children to draw a home, either one observed on a walk or one from a collection you have made, and ask them to label the features they recognise on their drawing. Discuss with them whether the features are older or modern.

A family at home in 1938

This photograph shows a family listening to the 'wireless' just before the outbreak of the Second World War. The wireless set, still a relatively new domestic item for many people at this time, proved to be an invaluable resource prior to, and during, the war. Families listened for information, propaganda and instructions as to what they must do. Here the family have gas masks and appear to be waiting for news of either the outbreak of war, or perhaps, a gas attack, since these were widely expected in the pre- and early war years. (Gas masks had been issued to everyone in 1938.)

The family's dress and the furniture in the room are significantly different from what we would see in a modern family home. An interesting feature of the photograph is the bed; perhaps the family were temporarily living in one room, which was protected against bombing raids and gas attacks, or maybe the wireless was in one of the bedrooms.

Children watching TV

This modern photograph of children watching television in their living room at home will provide children with an opportunity to compare one way in which everyday life has changed since the end of the 1930s. From the remote-controlled TV, to the comfortable chairs and carpets, many features of home life have clearly changed and can be noted by the children.

Details to do with the children in the picture also show changes, such as their hairstyles, clothes and even the fact that the boy is wearing a watch, commonplace now, but fairly rare in 1938.

Above all, the attitudes and expressions of those photographed is completely different. These children are relaxed and happy, in sharp contrast to the family in 1938, waiting with anxious expressions to hear if they are going to be attacked in some way.

Discussing the photographs

▶ Ask the children what they can see in the photographs. Who do they think the people are and what are the settings?

▶ Ask if they think the people in the photographs look different. In what ways are they different? Focus on comparing the hairstyles and clothes in each picture (the patterns and the father's knitted pullover in the older picture date it).

▶ Ask the children which of the rooms looks more comfortable. Why do they think this is? (Focus on the soft armchairs, the rug and colourful walls in the modern living room.)

▶ What do the children think the family in the 1938 picture are doing? What is the object they are sitting around? Explain about the early radio, that it was called a wireless, and how sometimes it might have been rather crackly and difficult to hear. Explain that people did not have televisions in those days.

▶ Ask what is different about the television in the modern picture compared with the old wireless. (For example, it is remote-controlled, it shows pictures in colour, it is clearer to listen to.)

▶ Ask if any of the children know what the people have in their laps and hands in the older picture. Ask if they have heard of gas masks before. Explain what these were for and why people were told they needed them at the beginning of the war (gas attacks had been carried out at the end of the First World War, and the government anticipated that they would be carried out again).

Activities

▶ Ask the children to locate both of the pictures on the timeline (photocopiable page 50).

▶ Ask what is different about the wireless in the 1938 picture and a modern radio. If possible, provide a small modern radio for the children to use in making their comparison and play an old wartime recording to compare the sounds.

▶ Compare the programmes the children watch on television now with the programmes that would have been broadcast on the wireless in 1938 (news, plays, hymns, sports reports, reports from abroad).

▶ Make a same/different chart and complete this as a class using the two pictures. Ask the children what they think the most important differences or changes have been.

▶ Ask the children to complete the writing frame 'A modern family and home' on photocopiable page 54.

Edwardian scullery

This is a photograph of the scullery of a home in Limehouse, East London, taken at the beginning of the 20th century. The sculleries of many poor homes across the country were similar to this. To cope with all the needs of what was probably a large family, there was a simple stoneware sink and an enamel bowl, while no water tap is visible. This may have been in the back yard, or maybe even in the street. Below the sink, there may have been a copper, where water was heated for washing clothes. Next to the sink, there appears to be a simple hot plate, heated by a fire from below. The cooking implements can be seen on the shelves above the sink. A towel, or shawl is hanging from a hook on the wall and a doll sits in the foreground on a chair. The walls will have been whitewashed and the floor may have been made of clay or quarry tiles. There will have been no form of heating in the scullery, which will have felt cold and damp when no washing or cooking were taking place.

Modern kitchen

This modern kitchen dates from around 2000. It is spacious and includes facilities for cooking, washing and storing food and equipment. It also has space for the family to eat at the kitchen table. A feature of this kitchen is the bright, cheerful colour scheme and the design for ease in cleaning and maintenance. The flooring is also designed for easy cleaning.

Discussing the photographs

▶ Ask the children to study the photographs. Ask what they think the photographs show. Explain that the old kitchen is called a *scullery*, because it is such a small room associated with the tiny rooms in old households that were attached to the kitchen and used for washing dirty dishes. The scullery maid would have been responsible for this task.

▶ Discuss in detail what the children can see in the 'Edwardian scullery', for instance the sink and bowl, the cooking place, the shelves. Encourage them to discuss as many objects as possible and to describe them. Do the same for the 'Modern kitchen'.

▶ Talk about the kind of activities that go on in kitchens, such as cooking, washing. Discuss with the class how these things are the same for both pictures, and how and where they would take place in each. Ask if they think one of the kitchens would be an easier place to cook and wash in.

▶ What kind of materials do the children think that things are made from in the modern kitchen? Comment on how the cupboard doors and the floor are so plain. Do they think it is easy to keep clean? Do they think the Edwardian scullery was easy to keep clean? Why not?

Activities

▶ Ask the children to place both pictures on the timeline on photocopiable page 50.

▶ Ask the children to look at the pictures of the two types of kitchen and compare them carefully. Using the word cards (photocopiable pages 43–5), ask the children to identify words to describe the kitchens, and ask them to suggest further descriptive terms.

▶ Get the children to think about what is different in the two pictures. List the differences that they notice. Make a word bank using some of the words they suggest.

▶ Collect as many different pictures of kitchens as possible, both present day and past. Ask the children to work in pairs or small groups to sort the pictures into either *old* or *modern*. Observe how effectively and accurately they achieve this. Discuss with them why they are making their decisions.

▶ Read the story 'Memories of an old lady' (photocopiable page 52) to the class.

▶ Give the children a copy of the writing frame 'Matching memories of an old lady' (photocopiable page 55) to complete.

Early vacuum cleaner

This vacuum cleaner from Edwardian times clearly needed two people to work it. Operated by hand, it appears to have been powered by bellows concealed within the table. The pipe and cleaning tools, however, are surprisingly similar to those which accompany modern vacuum cleaners. The maid is using the cleaner in the same way as a modern one, although it is debatable how effectively the vacuum is removing the dust from the carpet, despite the advertisement. Note the old money figure, 42 shillings, at the bottom of the advert.

Discussing the picture

▶ Look at the picture with the class and ask them if they know what the people are doing. Ask if they think this is a picture of people cleaning now or a long time ago. How can they tell? Ask for volunteers to explain what each person is doing.

▶ What can the children see that is the same as, and different from, a modern vacuum cleaner?

▶ Ask if there is anything else in the picture that tells us it was made a long time ago? (The clothes, the style of decoration in the house.)

▶ Explain to the children that this is one of the very earliest vacuum cleaners. Discuss what kind of tools were used before vacuum cleaners were invented, such as brushes, dustpans, carpet beaters, and what life would have been like for people who cleaned homes then.

Activities

See 'Modern vacuum cleaner', below, for activities comparing the two products.

Modern vacuum cleaner

This is a recent model of an electric vacuum cleaner. Its appearance is significantly different from the 'Early vacuum cleaner', but the principles for its operation and use are the same. More compact, lighter, and easy for one person to use, it can be wheeled around the house and carried to different places without difficulty, and of course runs on electricity. Additional tools are easily accessible. In fact, the emphasis of the design is for speed and ease of use.

Discussing the photograph

▶ Look closely at this picture of a modern vacuum cleaner with the children and ask them to identify the different parts of it. Ask the children why they think the cleaner has wheels.

▶ Ask for volunteers to explain what makes the cleaner work (an electric motor, electricity and so on). Discuss what must be done to start the machine.

▶ Also discuss the dangers of using electricity and explain clearly that the children must never try to use electrical implements on their own or without telling their parents or carers.

▶ Ask if anyone knows what the word *vacuum* means. Explain in simple terms how the creation of a vacuum enables the machine to suck air, and with it, dust and dirt, into a bag.

Activities

▶ Get the children to locate both pictures on the timeline (photocopiable page 50).

▶ Ask the class to compare both vacuum cleaners and make a list of all the things the children can see that are different about them. Then list the differences that cannot be seen, such as the way the modern machine is powered. Explain that the way the cleaner sucks up the dust is the same now as it was long ago, it is the way it is powered that has changed.

▶ Arrange for the home corner in the classroom to have a variety of brushes and dustpans for the children to 'clean' with. Discuss the difference made by using a vacuum cleaner.

Washboard

This advertisement for a new washboard dates from Edwardian times. The caption sums up what washday meant to many mothers or maidservants who had the chore of doing the family washing each week. Clothes and household linen were made from heavy fabrics on the whole in those days, so washing and drying them was a very arduous task. Working life was also harder and there was more manual labour than today, thus resulting in dirtier clothes. Not surprisingly, clothes were only washed once a week, but the job must have been harder because of this. Marks and dirt had to be physically rubbed away by hand, and the new invention of the washboard must have been wonderful at the time, since it did take some of the hard work out of washday.

Discussing the picture

▶ Ask the children what they think this woman is doing. Why is she doing the washing by hand? What are the objects called that she is using?

▶ Ask the children how they know that the picture was made a long time ago (the dress, the style of the washtub, the style of the lettering in the text).

▶ How long ago do they think people used to wash this way? (Relating it to before your grandmother's day will be a good way for them to gauge the time.)

▶ Ask the children if they can guess why the picture was made. Read the caption with them and discuss what it means. Explain that this is an advertisement, promoting a new invention to help with washing clothes.

Activities
See 'Modern washing machine', below.

Modern washing machine

This modern electric washing machine is, like the washboard in its time, designed to take the hard work out of washing. It is also designed to look smart, and to be small enough to fit into a space in the kitchen, to be easy to clean and fast and simple to use. It contains much of the most modern technology, being controlled by a microchip, which ensures the correct temperature, speed and length of wash once you have selected the correct cycle for your items. Many machines also dry the washing, so that the whole operation is very simple and does not take up very much time. Modern washing machines enable people to continue with other things while the washing almost does itself, a major change from Victorian and Edwardian times, when everything had to be done by hand, taking up at least one or two days every week to carry out what is now a relatively simple household chore.

Discussing the picture
▶ Ask the children to explain what this machine is called and what it is used for. Do they have one similar to it at home? Who uses it in their home? Discuss how it can be used by anyone to wash clothes and other household things.
▶ Ask for volunteers to explain what powers the machine and how it works. Emphasise the safety aspects and explain that it is not a machine for children to use, partly because it is electrical and partly because injuries could be caused by the movement of the machine.
▶ Ask why the children think that the drum inside the machine goes round and round. What happens to the washing as it does this?
▶ Ask how the children can tell that this picture is a modern one.

Activities
▶ Ask the children to locate the pictures on the timeline (photocopiable page 50).
▶ Compare the movement of washing in a modern washing machine with the use of the old-fashioned washboard. Explain that maybe the principle is the same – friction is needed to remove the dirt from the fabrics.
▶ Working with the whole class during a shared writing session, compose simple sentences about the two pictures, such as *The washboard looks hard to use*.
▶ Collect some old-fashioned washing equipment, if possible including a washboard. Large blocks of carbolic soap should be used for cleaning by hand, since detergents had not been invented when washboards were used. A large old-fashioned scrubbing brush could also be used. Allow the children time to play with the washing things and to experiment with washing different types of old clothes and fabrics. Try to ensure they wash some thick, heavy materials like cotton and linen to see how hard it was to clean and dry them.
▶ Who do the children think would have done the washing in Edwardian times? What did this mean for the time spent by women in the home? Discuss how anyone can do the washing today, and how the children's parents and carers can do other things while the washing is being done by the machine, including leaving the house.
▶ Read 'Memories of an old lady' (photocopiable page 52), noting its description of washing.

Candle

This candle and candleholder will give children an idea of how most homes were lit until relatively recently. It was not until the end of the 19th century that different forms of lighting, such as paraffin and gas, were used by most ordinary people. Although the electric light bulb was invented much earlier than this, it was not in general use in the 19th century, remaining the preserve of the aristocracy. Candles have been used, however, throughout the centuries, since pre-Roman times. The light given by candles is dim and flickering, and in the 18th and 19th centuries, elaborate candelabra were designed to hold large numbers of candles, which provided more light for homes with large rooms. Life in poor homes would have been quite

gloomy and shadowy, making it difficult to work during the hours of darkness. Additionally, candles were smelly and messy and required time and care to light and put out.

Discussing the picture
▶ What can the children see in the picture? What do they think it was used for?
▶ Can any of the children tell the class what candles are made from? Has anyone seen a candle being made? Discuss how handmade candles are made by pouring wax repeatedly over the cord which forms the wick. Make sure the children understand about the different parts of the candle, such as the wax, the wick, the candle holder.
▶ Ask if they can see what the candle holder in this picture is made from. How do they think it was made? Talk about how wood was 'carved' in the past using just a sharp knife.
▶ Discuss how effectively rooms could be lit by a candle. Ask what the children think happened in very large houses in the days of candlelight. (Explain how many candles were used together to light large rooms and tell them what candelabra are.)

Activities
See 'Modern electric lamps', below.

Victorian gas lamps

Lighting was much improved when the gas mantle was introduced. These gas mantles date from around 1888. A very common type of mantle was the one at the top of the picture, with adjustable chains. The lamp was lit by hand with a taper. The brightness of the light given off was adjusted by altering the amount of air admitted into the mantle by pulling the two chains to exactly the right position on either side of the mantle.

Gas lights were commonly used in middle-class homes in the latter part of the Victorian period. They were also used for street lighting at this time, as part of the improvements made by the late Victorians to public facilities (along with sewage and water systems, schools, hospitals, railways). Gas lights continued to be used well into the 20th century in working-class homes. Gas lights made a considerable difference to the quality of life of many people in late Victorian and early 20th-century times. Gas lamps also improved the safety of people going about their business in the streets, particularly in the dark nights of winter.

Discussing the picture
▶ Ask the children what they think the objects in the picture are, and what we call them. Have they seen any lamps like this before?
▶ Discuss how the lamps worked and what made the flame burn. Explain that they used gas, and that at one time only gas and candes were available. Explain to the children that gas can only burn if it has air around it. The little chains, shown on the lamp at the top, would be used to turn on or off the air, or to turn down the lamp so that it did not burn too brightly.
▶ Point out the glass covers over the flames on the lamps. Ask why these were used. (So the flame did not blow out and to prevent anyone burning themselves on an open flame.)

Activities
See 'Modern electric lamps', below.

Modern electric lamps

These anglepoise lamps are still popular forms of lighting for people working at their desks. They symbolise the developments in lighting at home and at work brought about by the use of electric power. Easy to use and designed to be manipulated to suit any working requirements, these lamps signalled a great step forward in the development of lighting.

Discussing the picture
▶ Ask the children to describe what they see in the picture. Ask what these items are and whether they have seen them before.
▶ Why do they think these modern lamps are designed in this way?
▶ Do they have lamps like these at home. If so, where are they used?
▶ How do the children think the lamps work and are powered?
▶ Can the children tell what these lamps are made from?

Activities

▶ Ask the children to locate each of the three types of lighting on the timeline (photocopiable page 50).

▶ Display the three pictures together at the front of the classroom, and ask the children to put them into chronological order. Discuss what each picture shows and how each type of lighting is more recent, or more modern, starting with the candle. Use the word cards on photocopiable pages 43–5 if appropriate.

▶ Ask the children to look at the pictures and explain what is different about each one, for example the different forms of energy used in each – fire, gas, electricity.

▶ Darken the classroom and light one candle. Discuss with the children how it must have felt to live in a home lit by only one or two candles. Let the children see how the wax melts and runs down into the holder. (Remind the children about the dangers of touching a lighted candle, including the hot wax, which can drip onto their hands.)

▶ Talk about the dangers that ordinary people must have faced when using candles in wooden, or thatched homes. (Remind the children that they must never try to light a candle or anything else when they are in or out of school. Stress the dangers of fire.)

▶ Read the story 'My sister' (photocopiable page 51) as an example of how gas lamps with chains were used.

▶ Ask the children to choose one form of lighting to draw and colour in detail, and then ask them to label it.

Victorian flat iron

The iron on the right hand side of the picture was known as a flat iron and, as the name suggests, it was made of solid iron and was very heavy. Flat irons were heated on an open fire or hot plate and were used in pairs, so that when the one in use cooled, it could be immediately exchanged for the second one from the fire. The handling of these very hot, heavy objects must have demanded considerable skill and dexterity, and must have resulted in many accidents.

The larger iron on the left-hand side of the picture is what is known as a 'slug iron'. It is taller than the earlier flat iron, with a hollow body, and has a wooden handle to resist the transmission of heat from the base. The slug iron was designed to remain hot for longer, without the need to keep replacing it on the fire. In an attempt to delay the cooling process, a heated piece of metal, or 'slug', would be inserted inside the iron, thus maintaining the heat for longer than the conventional flat iron. Sometimes, hot coals themselves would be put inside the iron to maintain its temperature, and kept inside by the use of a small door or flap, which was kept closed with a small latch on the outside. This can be seen at the back of the iron in the picture. In some areas of the world, such as parts of India, these irons are sometimes still in use, particularly in small villages where there is no electricity.

Modern steam iron

This modern iron represents a number of significant changes and developments in technology since the era of the flat iron. It is heated using electricity, which maintains the iron at any temperature that is required, for as long as required. The use of steam to assist in the ironing process is not a new idea, but has been incorporated here into the iron itself, for ease of use. The children can see the holes in the base of the iron where the steam is released onto the fabric. Before the steam iron was invented, steam was applied using a damp cloth to help remove stubborn creases or to iron particularly stiff, tough materials. This iron also has many safety features, such as a heat resistant body and handle. It is light and designed to be easy to use, unlike the very heavy, hot irons of the past.

Discussing the objects

▶ Compare the different kinds of iron in the pictures with the class. Ask the children what they think is different about them and what the main features of each type are.

▶ Discuss with the class what irons are used for and why.

▶ Discuss what each type of iron is made from. Can the children tell you how the materials used have changed?

▶ Ask the children if they know how the modern iron is heated, and how it remains hot while it is being used. Compare this with the flat iron; can they guess how this was heated?

▶ Now look at the 'slug iron'. Can any volunteers describe how they think this iron was heated? Explain that people began to think how they could keep irons hot long enough to finish their ironing, without having to constantly reheat them.

▶ Discuss how else irons have been heated in the past. For example, gas irons were used at one time, before electric ones.

▶ Ask the children which of the irons they think would be easier to use.

Activities

▶ Ask the children if they know how an iron is used. Get a volunteer to demonstrate with a modern iron, but one that is not plugged in. (Remind the children that they must not play with or use hot irons at home by themselves, as they can cause serious burns.)

▶ Print the pictures showing the different kinds of irons and display these together at the front of the classroom. Ask the children to put them into chronological order.

▶ Make a list of descriptive words on the board and create a word bank to assist the children in discussing the irons in a later activity. Include words such as *heavy*, *light*, *easy to use*, *hard to use*, *hot*, *cool*, *dangerous*, *safer*.

▶ Ask the children to choose one of the irons to draw in detail, and then get them to label their pictures using the words from the word bank on the board (see above).

▶ Look at the story 'My sister' (photocopiable page 51) with the children, focusing on how the maid used the flat irons.

Victorian water closet

This old-fashioned toilet was known as a water closet. The water closet was not commonly found inside the homes of ordinary people. In working-class homes, it was commonplace to have a row of houses with only one toilet between them. Some homes had a shared toilet at the bottom of the garden. It was not until the 20th century that hygiene improved sufficiently for toilets to be considered suitable for inclusion inside the house. For many people, even into the early 20th century, there was no access to a toilet like this one. Buckets or pails had to be used and emptied at night by the 'night soil' man, who came round with a cart. Such conveniences as a WC were very much the preserve of the well-to-do for most of the 19th century, and only gradually became accepted as a necessary part of the home in the mid-20th century. This water closet was made around 1900, and although displayed in a case, it is likely to have been removed from this when installed in a home. It has many similar features to a modern toilet, except that it has entirely wooden and metal fittings. One difference from most modern toilets is the placing of the water tank high up near the ceiling, and the chain used to flush the toilet, which is likely to have had a porcelain handle. The mechanism, however, is basically the same as that in a modern toilet. (Many types of water closet and modern toilets can be seen in a special gallery at the Gladstone Pottery Museum in Stoke-on-Trent.)

Modern toilet

In complete contrast, this modern toilet is designed to fit into any home. It is compact and designed for ease of cleaning. It has smooth lines and is deliberately designed in white for simplicity, with hygiene in mind. Although the flush mechanism is likely to be very similar to its Victorian counterpart, the toilet's external appearance is very different. The water tank is low and easy to reach for maintenance, and the toilet is flushed using a small lever instead of a chain. The toilet is designed to use much less water than earlier versions, in an effort to conserve shrinking water resources.

Discussing the pictures

▶ Compare the picture of the 'Victorian water closet' with the 'Modern toilet'. Ask the children if they have seen an old-fashioned toilet like the water closet. Some children may have toilets similar to these at home if they live in an old house.

▶ Ask the children what details tell us that one object is old and one is new. Encourage them to look at the materials used in each. Note that the older toilet is made of porcelain, wood and metal, while the new one is made of porcelain and plastic.

▶ Ask the class to compare how each toilet works, noting that the water flushes in just the same way, but that one has a chain and the other has a lever to make it flush. Ask if they have seen toilets with other ways of flushing, maybe when they have travelled to other countries.

▶ Explain how long ago, many people did not have toilets in their homes, and how in Victorian times there might only be one toilet for a whole street. Explain the problems experienced with public health before toilets were in common use, such as cholera and typhoid outbreaks where many people became ill or died. Stress the need for hygiene to keep us healthy.

Activities

▶ Discuss the different parts of each toilet, and make a list on the board of vocabulary suggested by the children.

▶ Ask the children to draw an old and a new toilet and to use this word list to label their drawings. Also draw upon the word cards on photocopiable pages 43–5.

▶ Using magazines, newspapers and catalogues, look for pictures of toilets from different times and make a collection of these pictures for a display.

▶ If possible, organise a visit to the Gladstone Pottery Museum in Stoke-on-Trent, where a complete history of toilets can be seen.

▶ Ask the children to locate the pictures on the timeline (photocopiable page 50).

NOTES ON THE PHOTOCOPIABLE PAGES

Word cards
PAGES 43–9

Two specific types of vocabulary have been introduced on the word cards:
▶ words related to the passing of time and chronology, such as *long ago* and *recent*
▶ descriptive vocabulary to help the children describe different homes, such as *detached house*, *flat*, and *bungalow*; or household objects, such as *iron* and *toilet*.
Encourage the children to think of other appropriate words to add to the descriptive terms in order to build up a word bank for the theme of homes. The word cards can be used during discussion and activities on the CD pictures and the stories. Children will also find it helpful to use the cards in displays and in writing captions for their pictures.

Activities

▶ Once you have made copies of the word cards, cut them out and laminate them, and use them as often as possible when talking about homes.

▶ Encourage the children to match the words to the pictures on the CD as often as possible. For example, provide printouts of pictures of groups of homes or household goods from the CD and ask the children to choose word cards that describe the features common to the group.

▶ Play pairing games with the children using sets of pictures printed from the CD and word cards, encouraging the children, with support, to match words and pictures. Children could work individually with an adult. Make a note of the children who can choose the right words.

▶ Begin to encourage the children, during whole class lessons, to think of sentences containing the key words they have learned to read. For example, *Long ago my grandparents lived in a house like this one.*

Timeline of homes
PAGE 50

The aim of this timeline is primarily to introduce young children to the idea of a sequence of events, presented in chronological order. No dates have been included, since these may prove confusing for many of the children who have not yet progressed to working with large numbers.

This timeline relates to the images of homes on the CD. It could be used at the beginning of a topic on homes in the past, to give children some visual representation of what we mean by *long ago* and *present day*. It could be adapted for the classroom in the form of a larger scale timeline for the wall, or as a long string which could be stretched across the classroom to represent the distance in time. Pictures could be substituted to show changes in homes, as the topic progresses. This kind of timeline is also useful at the end of a topic for checking, through the use of directed questioning, children's success in grasping ideas of sequence and chronology, and can be a useful assessment tool.

Discussing the timeline

▶ Before you start teaching the theme of homes, ask the class what they think this timeline shows.

▶ Discuss what we mean by *Victorian*.

▶ What does *Twentieth century* mean? Ask the children to give dates that are part of the twentieth century.

▶ Finally, discuss what *present* or *present day* means.

▶ Talk about how the past in Victorian times is different compared with other times in the past, like the 1950s, for example. Explain how periods in the past are all different from each other.

Activities

▶ Make a class timeline using this as an example. Ask the children to put on any relevant pictures they find in the appropriate places on the timeline.

▶ Add other periods to the timeline if the children have a good grasp of what it means and give them other sequencing tasks using these periods.

Stories about homes and household items

These stories are intended to be shared with the children in ways appropriate to your class. They may be read to the class in story time, or used in the shared reading time within the Literacy Hour. The stories might be used as a stimulus for shared writing about another kind of home or house. The theme could also be linked to work on the homes of people in other lands, or the homes of animals, birds or pets. Pictures on the CD will relate to the stories and can be used to illustrate them.

More able children could be encouraged to make up stories of their own to tell the rest of the class. These could form the beginning of a class collection of stories about homes and houses, which you might put together from suggestions from the children and their parents or carers.

My sister
PAGE 51

This story can be read in conjunction with the pictures of the 'Victorian gas lamps' and the 'Victorian flat iron' (provided on the CD). It provides a context for introducing these objects to young children, and also aims to develop their awareness of the dangers involved in using them. It could be read with the whole class in shared reading time, or with a group as a guided reading activity. More able readers might be able to read the story themselves, with the support of an adult. The historical content could then be discussed in more detail in a subsequent lesson. The story is set in a middle-class Victorian home, where servants are the norm, and the family has the luxury of a large drawing room. It contrasts with the experiences of children living in the poorer home described in the story 'Memories of an old lady' (photocopiable page 52). This type of story will be familiar to those children who have heard the *My Naughty Little Sister* stories of Dorothy Edwards, and these might also be used to introduce the children to a later period in time.

Discussing the story

▶ Ask the children how old they think the little sister is. (Point out that she can't be very old as she doesn't understand the dangers in what she is doing.)

▶ How can they tell that the things that happened in this story happened a long time ago?

▶ Ask for volunteers to explain why the little sister left the hot iron on the shirt.

▶ Do the children think the little sister understands how naughty she is being? Do they think that perhaps she is just playing at doing the maid's work?

▶ Why does the narrator refer to her *father* rather than her *dad*?

Activities

▶ Look with the children at other pictures of objects from Victorian or Edwardian homes. Challenge them to think what other silly things a naughty sister might have done with some of them, and ask them to begin writing their own short stories.

▶ Show the children pictures and drawings of rooms from middle-class Victorian homes. As them what other objects they can see that are different from things in their own homes.

Memories of an old lady

PAGE 52

This is a story for you to read and share with the whole class, or with a group of children. It can be read alongside the picture of the 'Edwardian scullery' and the 'Washboard' (provided on the CD). The story aims to put these pictures into a setting that the children will understand. It seeks to convey the hard work involved in washday, and the difficulties faced by poor people living in homes with very few facilities at the turn of the 20th century. It also enables the children to empathise with the experiences of children living in such homes, since it is told from the perspective of childhood memories.

Discussing the story

▶ Show the children the picture of the 'Edwardian scullery' while telling them this story. As you describe life in the scullery, get the children to notice the objects you are talking about.
▶ Discuss with the children what any new words mean, such as *grumble*, *boiled food*, *stew*.
▶ Talk to the children about the *copper*. What do they think this is?
▶ Ask the children whether they think it was enjoyable living in the old lady's childhood home. Do they think it was always difficult?

Activities

▶ Provide the children with the word cards on photocopiable pages 43–5, 48 and 49, and ask them to make up sentences using these words about life in an Edwardian scullery.
▶ Write the beginning of a sentence from the story on the board, such as *There was no bath...* Ask for volunteers to complete the sentence, remembering what was in the story.
▶ Use the writing frame 'Matching memories of an old lady' (photocopiable page 55) with the class.

Writing/drawing frames

These vary in difficulty, from simple tasks which include opportunities for drawing for less able readers and writers, to more challenging reading and more demanding tasks for those children who may need extension work. Nevertheless, less able readers may be assisted in completing all the writing frames with support from an adult, or perhaps by working as a pair with a more able reader. Many of the writing frames could also be completed as part of a whole class shared writing activity.

Old and new vacuum cleaners

PAGE 53

This writing and drawing frame will need to be used in conjunction with the pictures of the 'Early vacuum cleaner' and the 'Modern vacuum cleaner' (provided on the CD), to assist the children in their drawing. It will need to follow discussion about the different cleaners, about how each one works and their similarities and differences. The vocabulary also needs to have been incorporated into the preceding discussion.

A modern family and home

PAGE 54

This writing frame needs to be used following discussion of the pictures of 'A family at home in 1938' and 'Children watching TV' (provided on the CD). Vocabulary to describe the two pictures needs to have been introduced before giving the children the task of completing the writing frame. Model how to use the frame, giving one or two examples if necessary.

Matching memories of an old lady

PAGE 55

This writing frame is intended for use in conjunction with the 'Edwardian scullery' picture (provided on the CD) and with the story 'Memories of an old lady' (photocopiable page 52). It is a fairly challenging task, requiring good reading ability and grammar sense if it is to be completed by children working individually. Less confident readers will need to work in pairs or with the support of an adult.

Time-sequencing word cards

new

newer

newest

old

older

oldest

before

after

long ago

modern

recent

old-fashioned

Time word cards (2)

when my parents were children

when my carer was a child

when my grandparents were young

Types of home word cards

home	**house**
flat	**bungalow**
terraced house	**detached house**
semi-detached house	**caravan**

◀SCHOLASTIC
PHOTOCOPIABLE

Features of homes word cards

chimney
window
sash window
window panes
doorway
porch

Rooms in homes word cards

kitchen

living room

bathroom

bedroom

scullery

◼ SCHOLASTIC PHOTOCOPIABLE

Household word cards

vacuum cleaner

washtub

candle

cooker

iron

toilet

Timeline of homes

Victorian times

Twentieth century

Present day

My sister

Children in my day were supposed to be very very good, but my little sister was sometimes a naughty girl. She played with things that she was not allowed to touch. She was only very small, but she did some silly things.

One day, when it was getting dark, the maid had lit the gas lights and lamps in the drawing room. My naughty sister waited until she had left the room and pulled all the chains first one way, then the other, to make the lamps and lights very dim. Father came into the room and tripped over a chair because it was so dim.

My sister loved to watch the maid working at the ironing. This was a hard job, working with the heavy, hot, flat irons. One day, when the maid had finished and had left the irons to cool, my naughty sister thought she would do some ironing too. She picked up the heavy iron and managed to lift it onto one of Father's white shirts. But she could not lift it again to take it off and it was still quite hot. So my little sister left it and went away to play with her dolls. You can guess what happened. When the maid came back, there was a dreadful burning smell, and a large hole in Father's shirt!

Memories of an old lady

Now I am a very old lady. I am 95 years old, but I can still remember the things my mother used to do when I was a child. We lived in a small terraced house, which had been built in Victorian times. There were six children in our family. My mother found it difficult to keep us all clean and fed, because we did not have a lovely kitchen like people have today. All we had was a tiny scullery at the back of the house. There was no bath, no modern toilet or a modern sink. We just had a stone sink with a bowl to wash in. On Saturday night, we all used to have a bath in an old tin bath in front of the fire in the living room. We only had one living room, so everything had to be done in there.

My mother had to cook on a small hot plate in the scullery. She used to grumble about trying to light the fire under it, especially on wet days, when it was hard to light. We often had boiled food and stew because it was hard to cook anything else. She also had to light a fire to heat water in the copper when she had to wash all our clothes by hand. I remember she used to be in a bad mood on Sunday nights when she began to soak the dirty clothes. She had to spend two or three days washing and drying everything. She used to be very tired at the end of it all. Then the following week, it would all begin again.

◣ SCHOLASTIC
PHOTOCOPIABLE

Old and new vacuum cleaners

△ Draw a picture of an early vacuum cleaner and a modern vacuum cleaner. Find the right words to describe each one and write them below your pictures.

hand-operated   wooden

old   electric   plastic   new

A modern family and home

▷ Choose words to describe a modern family and home from the list at the bottom of the page.

Things that we might see in a modern family and home.

gas masks		television	
pullover	jeans		wireless
remote control		bright colours	
patterned dresses		soft armchairs	

Matching memories of an old lady

▷ Match the beginnings and endings of the sentences. Write out the complete sentences when you have matched them up.

Beginnings

We had a tiny scullery

We just had a stone sink

We all used to have a bath

She had to light a fire

She had to wash

Endings

to heat water in the copper.

with a bowl to wash in.

in an old tin bath in front of the fire.

all our clothes by hand.

at the back of the house.

HOLIDAYS

Content, skills and concepts

This chapter links to Unit 3 of the QCA Scheme of Work for history at Key Stage 1, 'What were seaside holidays like in the past?', and so focuses on the theme of holidays. It can be used to assist teachers in planning, resourcing and meeting the objectives set for this unit. Together with the Holidays Resource Gallery on the CD-ROM it includes a range of resources, both visual and written, which can be used in teaching this unit. Like the QCA unit, the chapter looks at seaside holidays in the past. It provides materials to support the teaching of similarities and differences between holidays today and holidays in the past. Oral history, discussion and the sorting and description of objects are all prior learning activities which will have introduced relevant skills and concepts to the children in the Foundation Stage, before they progress to the skills and concepts in this unit.

Resources on the CD-ROM

Pictures of holiday resorts and beaches, souvenirs and holiday advertisements from the past and present are provided on the CD-ROM. Teacher's notes containing background information about these sources are provided in this chapter. Also on the CD-ROM is a film of an interview with a grandparent talking about her memories of holidays in the 1930s. This will involve the children with real-life experiences from the past, in what is both an accessible and engaging format for the young child. The video can be used as a resource and as a stimulus for talking and writing.

Photocopiable pages

Photocopiable resources can be found within the book and are also provided in PDF format on the CD-ROM, from which they can be printed. They include:
▶ a timeline
▶ word cards which highlight the essential vocabulary of this topic
▶ stories and non-fiction texts about holidays
▶ writing and drawing frames
The teacher's notes that accompany all the photocopiable text resources include suggestions for ways of using the pages for whole class, group or individual activities.

Stories and non-fiction texts

The stories and texts are designed to both interest the children in the pictures from the CD, and also to introduce them to notions of the past and present. They have been written at different reading levels. This will enable teachers to use them for shared reading or as part of a guided reading session. Very able readers may be able to read one of the simpler stories, with support from an adult.

History skills

Skills such as observing, describing, sorting, sequencing, comparing, inferring, listening, speaking, reading, writing and drawing are involved in the activities provided in the teacher's notes for both the resources on the CD and in the book. For example, in looking at pictures of old and modern seaside holidays, the children will observe closely the differences between the two. They can learn to use descriptive vocabulary to describe and compare the different seaside holidays. They will listen to a story and perhaps be involved in sharing the reading of the story. They can then work on the suggested activities and complete the writing frames provided, which also involve some scaffolded writing.

Historical understanding

In the course of the suggested tasks, a further overarching aim is for children to begin to develop their notions of old and new, the past and of the passing of time. They will begin to understand that things are different in some ways from things in the past, but in other ways, the same. They will also develop an awareness that there are different times in the past, and that these were also different from each other.

NOTES ON THE CD-ROM RESOURCES

Major seaside resorts in the British Isles

This outline map of the British Isles shows the major seaside resorts as they are today. It is for use when discussing the children's memories of their own seaside holidays. They can try to locate on the map the places they have been on holiday, or these places can be added to the map if they are not already included. Words such as *north*, *south*, *east*, *west* can be introduced, along with vocabulary such as *coast*, *bay*, *beach*, *ocean*, *resort*.

Discussing the map

▶ Explain to the children that it is a map of the British Isles. Check that they know what countries this includes.
▶ Read through the names of some of the seaside places on the map. Ask the children if they can read any out.
▶ Ask if anyone has been on holiday to any of the places on the map.
▶ Ask if any children have been on holiday in the British Isles, but the place is not on the map. Locate where it is and then add it to the map.
▶ Why do they think people like to go to the coast for their holiday?

Activities

▶ Identify the children who have visited seaside resorts shown on the map. Ask them to put stickers on the places they have been and to say a little about what they did there.
▶ Ask the class to make a list of words which describe seaside holidays and the things they like about the seaside. Record these on the board.
▶ Use the map in conjunction with pictures of Brighton on the CD, such as 'Modern Brighton beach' or 'The bathing machine'. Display the map in the centre of a large board and link with lines or threads the place name on the map to the pictures of Brighton. If children can bring in pictures of resorts they have visited on holiday, add these to the display too. Include appropriate vocabulary from the word cards (photocopiable pages 71–3) and words the children have suggested.

Modern family by the sea

This image shows some key aspects of how a family might appear on the beach today. They wear very casual clothes, with those of the parents and children similar in appearance. They make use of a large amount of equipment at the beach. Father has a body board, a popular beach accessory, along with surf boards. The children have a beach ball, a spade and a rake. The emphasis in the picture is on both enjoyment and fitness. This has been a theme of seaside holidays since Victorian times, that of going to the sea for one's health.

Discussing the picture

▶ Ask whether the children think these are modern people, or people from the past. Ask how they know this. What are the clues they are using to decide?
▶ What can they say about the children's clothes in the picture? Are they like the clothes they wear on the beach? What do they notice about the clothes of the parents? Do these look modern? Why? (Is it because their parents also wear clothes like these?)
▶ Ask the children if they can suggest how the people in the picture feel – do they look happy?

Activities

▶ Ask the children to locate the picture on the timeline (photocopiable page 74).
▶ During a shared writing session with the whole class, make a list of words about beach toys and games, such as *bucket*, *spade*, *beach ball*, *cricket*.
▶ Provide materials for the children to draw pictures of their favourite beach toys.
▶ Provide the writing frame 'My favourite holiday' (photocopiable page 80) for the children to complete in pairs or independently.
▶ Show the children the interview 'Seaside holidays when I was young' (provided on the CD). Ask the children: *What things did Sheila play with, and do, on the beach?*

1950s swimwear

Models posing in this photograph illustrate typical beachwear for ladies in the 1950s. Taken in 1958, the photograph shows how these costumes were still reminiscent of the fuller styles of earlier times. They are designed as short skirts or are full and puffy, and are well supported with shoulder or neck straps. One even includes a matching stole for covering the shoulders. Impeccable hairstyles were also of great importance in this period, so ladies and girls were expected to wear rubber bathing hats whenever they went into the water, either in a swimming pool or the sea. As can be seen, the men in the background do not seem to have been encumbered while swimming with the same requirements. Styles for men's beachwear have probably changed less than those for women over the years.

Discussing the picture

▶ Ask the class if they think this is a modern photograph or an old-fashioned one. What are the clues that tell us this? (The children may assume it is modern because it is in colour.)
▶ See if the children can guess the date of the picture, or how long ago it was taken. Tell them that it was taken in 1958. Discuss how many years ago this is.
▶ Ask the children why they think the ladies look rather unusual to us today, for example the way they are posing for the photograph. Discuss how these women are known as *models* and how they are probably modelling new beachwear for 1958. Ask *Do you think that models would pose like this today?*
▶ Do the children like the swimming costumes? Would they be easy to swim in?
▶ What are the models in the water holding in their hands? Why did they have these?

Activities

See 'The bathing machine', below.

Victorian beachwear

Most people in this scene are fully dressed in their everyday suits and long dresses, although they are on the beach. Both men and women are still wearing their hats, some ladies carry parasols. It is difficult to see the kind of swimwear worn by adults and this was intentional. Bathing machines were drawn up close to the water's edge so that the occupant could descend directly into the water, unseen by other people. The children playing on the beach appear to be wearing one-piece suits with trouser legs, and some with sleeves. Men wore similar bathing suits, while women's swimming costumes were similar to shortened versions of their normal dress, with skirts and sleeves that must have been quite difficult to swim in. While sea bathing was considered to be a healthy pursuit, it was still considered unseemly for a lady to be seen with any part of her body uncovered, even in late Victorian times.

Discussing the picture

▶ Discuss what can be seen in this picture with the class.
▶ Ask the children what kind of picture it is (a photograph). Is it like a modern photograph? What is different about it?
▶ How many people can they see dressed for swimming? Where are these people?
▶ Can they see any adults in swimsuits on the beach? How are most of the grown-ups dressed on the beach? Why do they think this is?
▶ Talk about the bathing machines, seen on the left of the picture. Explain what they were for, and why they were used.
▶ Do the children think the people enjoyed being dressed in these heavy clothes on the beach?

Activities

See 'The bathing machine', below, for activities using all three beachwear images.

The bathing machine

In this illustration we can see how the Victorian bathing machine was used. Rather like a cart in its construction, the bathing machine was made so that it could be wheeled to the water's edge when needed. There was a door at the front and another at the back. The occupant could enter the machine from the sand, change into her beach attire and enter the water

without being seen by anyone else on the beach. Having taken their bathe, the occupant would change into her daywear and re-emerge on the beach side of the machine, fully dressed. Only the heads and arms of other women swimming in the sea can be seen.

The boy in the foreground wears a sailor suit with matching sailor hat, a popular style at the time for children.

Discussing the picture

▶ Ask the class what kind of picture they think this is (a drawing). How do they know?

▶ Ask the children what they think is happening in the picture. Explain that the object they can see is called a bathing machine, and tell them what it was used for.

▶ See if the children can guess how the bathing machine worked. Ask: *How is it that this lady is appearing fully dressed whilst being so close to the water's edge?*

▶ Discuss Victorian attitudes about dress, and explain how people were not allowed to appear in public unless they were fully dressed in their long clothes. Explain how the bathing machine was very popular because it allowed everyone to go swimming in the sea if they wanted to (and if they had money for one).

Activities

▶ Compare the pictures '1950s swimwear', 'Victorian beachwear' and 'The bathing machine', and ask the children to explain how people looked different in the two periods of time that they show.

▶ Challenge the children to put the pictures 'Victorian beachwear' and '1950s swimwear' into chronological order.

▶ Complete as part of a shared writing session, the 'Old and new holidays' writing frame (photocopiable page 79), recording the similarities and differences about two of the pictures.

▶ Show the children the interview 'Seaside holidays when I was young' (provided on the CD). Focus in particular on the part where Sheila talks about the clothes she used to wear in the 1930s, and on the photographs of Sheila as a child.

▶ Read 'Toby on the beach' (photocopiable page 77) and ask the children when they think the story is set. How can they tell?

Brighton beach (1890)

This photograph of a beach scene, taken in 1890, shows many typical features of the Victorian seaside. There are numerous small boats, conspicuous with their large white sails. Bathing machines, used for people to change before venturing into the water, are lined up along the water's edge. The people walking on the beach or along the promenade are all very formally dressed, in heavy-looking, long clothes, with both men and women wearing hats. Benches are available on the beach for anyone who wishes to sit and admire the view. The pier can be seen in the distance. There is evidence of organised amusements, such as the advertisement for a regatta on a billboard in the foreground.

The idea of seaside holidays was new in late Victorian times and although people took readily to the idea, they were slow to adapt their attitudes and way of life, seen in their style of dress and reluctance to be seen in bathing costumes.

Discussing the picture

▶ Ask the children if they think the picture is a painting, drawing or photograph.

▶ What is it a photograph of? What clues can they find that tell them this?

▶ Ask the children to look closely at the picture. If possible, give them copies of the picture to share, while working in pairs. They might enjoy using magnifiers to find small details.

▶ Make a list on the board of the things the children notice. Read the words through with the class.

▶ What can the children see in the distance, in the middle of the picture? What is it called? Have they ever been on a pier?

▶ Ask if there are any unusual things in the picture, or things they have not seen before, for example the goat in the foreground, the large sails on the boats, the bathing machines. Make a list of these, and discuss them.

Activities

See 'Modern Brighton beach', below, for activities comparing the two photographs.

Modern Brighton beach

Many features of present day Brighton appear unchanged since earlier times in this modern photograph. The pier is still there in this recent photograph, although it has since collapsed; the sailing boats are still lined up along the waterfront, although there are fewer than in the Victorian picture. There are still people sitting on the beach admiring the view and others walking along the promenade enjoying the sea air. However, there is also evidence of considerable development. The whole area appears to have been built up to a greater extent. There is a walled area for activities, such as boules or volleyball. The major change is in the creation of a large café area with seats and tables for people to relax and enjoy a drink or an ice cream next to the beach. Children will notice the colourfulness of this scene compared with the Victorian picture. While much of this difference is due to the earlier black and white photography, some features are in reality more colourful today than they were in Victorian times, such as the sails, the clothes people wear, the umbrellas in the café.

Discussing the picture
▶ Ask the children what kind of picture this is. How was it made?
▶ Ask if anyone has ever been to Brighton. Do they recognise things in this picture? Are the things they see similar to other resorts they may have visited?
▶ Get the children to identify the things they can see, such as the pier, the boats.
▶ Discuss how a day at the seaside is exciting for people who live inland. Discuss why this is, and why people want to go to the beach.

Activities
▶ Look together at the pictures 'Brighton beach (1890)' and 'Modern Brighton beach'. Ask the children to complete 'Old and new holidays' on photocopiable page 79.
▶ Comparing the two pictures, discuss and explain what the main changes and developments have been over the last 100 years, such as the influence from the continent in the form of 'café culture'; the new style and materials used in sails; building materials and clothes.
▶ Collect books about seaside holidays, now and in the past. Make these available for children to browse through in their spare moments.
▶ Use a wider variety of seaside pictures from the Holidays Resource Gallery on the CD from different times in the past. Challenge the children to put them into chronological order and to explain how they have made their decisions.
▶ Make a large wall timeline, using photocopiable page 74 to start you off. Get the children to put the pictures in the above activity into the right places on the timeline. Discuss the way seaside holidays have changed by looking at the timeline together.
▶ Provide a wide variety of objects from the seaside for the children to use in observational drawing, or use 'Starfish', 'Shell', 'Lollipop' and 'Sand bottle' (provided on the CD).

Victorian map of Brighton

Although made in 1908, this map still shows Brighton very much as it was in late Victorian times. It shows very similar streets and houses to the present day, since these have changed very little since Victorian times. The railway line and station are already there, along with the public parks, like Queen's Park, The Level and St Anne's Well gardens. What is surprising, is how many amenities and places of entertainment are already developed. For example, the aquarium is there (referred to as the sealife centre on the modern map), both piers are present and also the electric railway. However, some features of modern life are as yet not present on the map, such as road numbers and disabled facilities.

Modern map of Brighton

This map shows central Brighton as it is today, along with the main beaches and the piers. Features such as the Brighton Centre and the Entertainment Centre appear on it, along with the modern Churchill Square Shopping Centre. Bus and railway stations are clearly marked. A particular feature of note is the indication of facilities in several parts of the town for disabled people. Another modern feature of the map is the numbering of the roads, for example the A259, an indication of the prime importance of road transport in the 20th and 21st centuries.
To view the map most clearly, choose the 'Print using Acrobat' option on screen.

Discussing the maps
▶ Show the children the two maps of Brighton together. Discuss what the maps show, such as where the beach is and where the streets are.
▶ Ask what they can see that is different about the two maps.
▶ Explain that they are both maps of Brighton, but that one is a modern map and the other is a much older, Victorian map. Ask the children which map they think is older. Encourage the children to look for clues to help them decide which is an old and which is a new map. (For example, the old map shows fewer buildings and streets.)

Activities
▶ Give each child a copy of both maps and ask them to mark on the modern map where and how the town has changed and grown.
▶ Ask the children to draw a simple map of their route to school. They can check this at home with their parents and then bring in a more detailed version for the next lesson.

Excursion advertisement (1902)

Published in the year following the death of Queen Victoria, this advertisement for an excursion by train to the coast is an example of how train travel changed the lives of ordinary people. From late Victorian times, train travel became gradually more popular and accessible to the general public, and cheap returns of this kind, in third class accommodation, were accessible even to the working classes. Such travel not only widened opportunities for leisure and employment, but also contributed to the growth of seaside resorts such as Brighton, featured in this example. The aged, browned paper, old-fashioned lettering and money will all be of interest to young children.

Discussing the picture
▶ Ask the children to guess what the picture shows. What clues can they use to help them identify this? (The dates, lists of train times, fares, the main title.)
▶ Ask what they notice about the typeface. Is it like modern lettering?
▶ What other clues can the children find to tell them that the picture is old? Talk about the faded paper and the way the advertisement is written, for example *Will run as under*. What does this mean? What might we write nowadays?
▶ What do the children notice about the costs of the trips? Discuss the fact that the fares are shown in old money, such as shillings and pence.
▶ Ask what the children notice about the times of the trips. Would they like to start a trip at five o'clock in the morning? Why do the children think that the journey had to start so early? (Trains were slower; they may have stopped more often.)
▶ Ask if anyone has ever been on a train journey to the seaside. What was it like? Describe your own experiences if the children have never been on a train.

Activities
▶ Make a collection of modern examples of advertisements for day trip excursions to the seaside on trains or buses.
▶ Compare these with the 'Excursion advertisement (1902)' picture. Discuss the differences you can see. Look at the things that are the same.
▶ Read *Come away from the water, Shirley* by John Burningham (Red Fox). Discuss the story with the children. Talk about the adventures Shirley had and how long the family were on the beach. Find other stories about the seaside and discuss them with the class.
▶ Provide an outline template of an advertisement and challenge the children, working in pairs, to complete the details.

Edwardian postcard

This souvenir postcard is valuable in the way it illustrates not only ladies' bathing costumes during the late Victorian/early Edwardian period, but also the prevailing attitudes amongst the older generation at that time. The long skirts, trousers and sleeves incorporated into early bathing costumes reflect the views of the age, when ladies were expected never to reveal their arms or legs. It is interesting to note that the younger girls in the picture have shorter sleeves and lower necklines in their bathing suits, as well as failing to wear a bathing cap, worn by the older lady. The bathing machines (see page 58), seen in the background here, were designed to enable ladies to change and enter the water unseen, hence, no doubt, Mamma's annoyance at the presence of a man in the water nearby.

Discussing the postcard

▶ Ask the children what they think this item was used for. Ask if it reminds them of anything they have seen at the seaside.

▶ Tell the children that these kinds of postcards are kept as souvenirs. Discuss the meaning of the word *souvenir*. Ask what kind of souvenirs they bring home from their holidays.

▶ Do the children send postcards when they are on holiday? Do they ever receive any? What type of pictures do they have on them today?

▶ Ask the children if they can work out from looking at the details when the picture was made, for example the bathing machines and the style of dress.

▶ Was the postcard was meant to be serious or funny. Discuss the caption, and whether this was a kind of joke. (You may need to explain some background to bathing at the time.)

Activities

▶ Ask the children to locate the picture on the timeline (photocopiable page 74).

▶ Collect some modern seaside postcards which make jokes about people in the water or on the beach. Ask the class to compare these with this Edwardian example, and discuss the similarities and differences between them.

▶ Carry out a vote to decide which postcard the children think carries the funniest joke.

▶ Challenge the children to make up some jokes of their own and to illustrate them.

▶ During shared writing, make a list of the features in the 'Edwardian postcard' picture that are humorous. Discuss how the artist has made the picture funny.

Hove poster

This poster advertising Hove shows how over the years, attitudes gradually changed. By the 1930s, women had become far more emancipated and were beginning to compete in some aspects of life, such as swimming, alongside their male counterparts. Here, swimwear has become more serviceable for anyone actually wishing to swim! Although still with short legs, the swimsuit now enabled women to move more freely and suggests that older attitudes regarding what was appropriate dress had begun to break down by this time. Male and female swimwear had, in fact, become very similar. This new freedom is exemplified in the poster by the beach ball, suggesting that women could now also participate in beach games.

Discussing the poster

▶ Discuss the kind of picture this is with the class. Do they think it was drawn, painted or photographed? How do the children know?

▶ What do the children notice about the style of the lettering and the style of the artwork?

▶ Can the children recognise how the appearance of the lady in the picture has changed, compared with earlier times in the past, such as pictures of Victorian bathers?

▶ Tell the children about the changes that took place in women's lives at the beginning of the 20th century, such as being able to vote, get the same kind of education as men, wear a greater variety of clothes than in the past.

Activities

▶ Make a class sequence line, with no dates on, just pictures. You could use pictures from the CD, such as 'Modern family by the sea', '1950s swimwear' and 'Victorian beachwear'. Challenge volunteers to find an appropriate place for this picture on it. Discuss how they know that it is not modern, and how they also know that it is not Victorian.

▶ What is the purpose of the poster? Discuss how it encourages people to visit Hove.

▶ Find Hove on a map of the British Isles. Establish why it is popular as a seaside resort.

▶ Look at the beach ball the woman is holding, and ask if the children have beach balls at home. Ask the children to design patterns for modern beach balls.

▶ Compare this picture with swimwear from other times, using the pictures 'Modern family by the sea', '1950s swimwear' and 'Victorian beachwear' (provided on the CD). Ask them to sequence the pictures.

Sand bottle

Popular for many decades with children, souvenirs such as this bottle of coloured sand have been widely sold in seaside resorts. Areas like the Isle of Wight have specialised in these items for many years, because of the presence of many different coloured sands on the island's beaches and cliffs. The various colours in the sands there have been created over a long period of time from sedimentary rock – red, brown and grey sandstone, chalk and different coloured clays, including the so-called 'blue slipper'.

Discussing the picture
▶ Ask the children what they think this is, and why it is part of a collection of pictures about the seaside. Remind them of the word *souvenir*.
▶ Ask if they have ever looked in souvenir shops and seen things like this. Find out if anyone has a bottle or other container of coloured sand, and see if they can bring it to school for the class to see.
▶ Discuss how coloured sands came to exist and why they are interesting to us now, and especially to geologists. Ask if they think the sand in this picture is naturally this colour or if it has been dyed.
▶ Ask if the colours remind them of other multicoloured things, such as a rainbow. Discuss the names of the different colours and shades.

Activities
▶ Provide a range of different colouring media and ask the children to design their own sand bottles. Make a display of the pictures, alongside examples of any bottles of sand that have been brought in.
▶ Provide different coloured sands for the children to use in their free play time.
▶ Give opportunities for the children to experiment freely with colours in paint, oil pastels, and other mediums, or perhaps in drawing rainbows.
▶ During shared writing, make a list of all the 'colour' words the children know. Write some sentences on the boards about the colours they can see in the sand bottle.

Starfish

Found in many seaside resorts, starfish like this are popular souvenirs. Their shape and varied colours attract the attention of children and adults alike. Many starfish have a spiny skin, which acts like a spine. The starfish has five limbs. It moves slowly, but it can be agile when necessary. It can right itself if turned upside down in the water and prise open mussel and scallop shells. The starfish has no head or brain, but the arms have a sensory tentacle with an 'eye' at the tip that is sensitive to light. It has hundreds of tube feet on its limbs that can act as suction cups, giving it very fine motor control. If a starfish loses a limb, it is able to grow a new one. Children will enjoy talking about any starfish they have found and bringing them into school to share with the rest of the class.

Discussing the picture
▶ Ask the children if they have seen one of the creatures in the picture. Ask if they know what it is called. If the children are unsure, explain what a starfish is.
▶ Explain how starfish move in the water and what particular things they can do, such as growing new limbs.
▶ Discuss how they can be bought in souvenir shops. What do the children think about this? Point out that these creatures were once alive and that all creatures should be treated with care and respect.

Activities
▶ Encourage the children to read about starfish in either a shared or guided reading session.
▶ Make a collection of books about seashore life, seashells and so on, and encourage the children to look at these and talk about what they have found. If there are any pictures of starfish, group them according to the different types.
▶ Provide the children with drawing and colouring materials and ask them to draw a starfish, either copying one they have brought in, one from a book or using the picture from the CD.
▶ Make a class book of starfish, to include the children's pictures and captions.

▶ The non-fiction text 'Starfish' (photocopiable page 76) provides facts about starfish. Read it with the children in a discussion session on the picture.

▶ Use the story 'Saving the starfish' (photocopiable page 77) to enhance the children's knowledge of how starfish live using a more creative context.

Shell

Occasionally, children will be able to find good examples of these distinctive scallop shells on their holiday beaches. They will be able to talk about the pleasures of hunting on the sands until they come across a good example.

Scallops are found on all coasts of the British Isles. They like to live about 100 metres offshore in hollows in sand or fine gravel. The scallop shell is ribbed and thick and solid, and is often used for decorative purposes. The king scallop can grow up to 150 millimetres long. Scallops are active swimmers. They glide through the water and over the sea floor by snapping their shells together. They can also use this technique to squirt water at another sea creature that may be threatening them. These shells are probably best known for their colours and beautiful fan shape. They have been represented in works of art by many famous artists, such as Titian and Botticelli. Buildings in ancient Roman times were sometimes decorated with scallop shell ornaments.

Discussing the picture
▶ Ask if the children have seen anything like this object in the picture. What is it?
▶ Ask if anyone knows its particular name (scallop).
▶ Ask if they know which part of the sea creature can be eaten. Ask if anyone has ever eaten a scallop and whether they enjoyed it.
▶ Ask what other shellfish they have heard of. Which ones have they eaten?
▶ Discuss and explain how seafood was very fashionable in the past and was sold on stalls. (For example, cockles, mussels and winkles were very popular in Victorian and Edwardian times, and were still common at resorts until the 1950s. It may have been the onset of more serious pollution that has brought this tradition to an end.)

Activities
▶ Ask the children to draw around a cut-out version of the picture on the CD, or around a real shell, to make the shape. They could also make imprints of shell shapes in Plasticine, sand or wet plaster of Paris. These can then be coloured in when dry.
▶ Provide outline drawings of Ancient Roman bowls or buildings, which were often decorated with scallops, for the children to decorate using the scallop shell design.
▶ Ask the class to bring in any shell souvenirs they have for a class display. This could be organised on a sand tray. Help the children to label their shells and to write simple descriptions of them.
▶ In a shared reading session, read the non-fiction text 'The scallop shell' (photocopiable page 78) with the children to deepen their understanding of the picture.

Lollipop

Sticks of rock have always been one of the most popular souvenirs from British seaside resorts. More recently, these have been overtaken by more modern sweets, such as the giant sugar walking stick and giant coloured lollipops or dummies. Along with holiday photographs and seashells, these are things that young children treasure and remember from their seaside holidays. Whether any remain to be brought into school is another question!

Discussing the picture
▶ Ask the children what they can see in the picture. Have they seen a lollipop like this before? Where? (They can usually be found in sweet or souvenir shops at the seaside.)
▶ Discuss the different colours in the lollipop and ask the children to give their names. Make a list of these on the board, and ask for volunteers to read as many as they can.
▶ Discuss what kind of things children a long time ago, in Victorian or Edwardian times, might have eaten at the seaside. Would they have had sweets like this? Explain why not.
▶ Discuss with the children what people would have eaten as a treat at the seaside in the past, such as cockles, mussels, whelks, oysters, jellied eels.

Activities

▶ Set up, as a structured play area, a seaside souvenir shop, or a sweet shop, selling all kinds of seaside confectionery.

▶ Find pictures of old-fashioned foods that were eaten at the seaside. Get the children to make posters of these, advertising them as treats.

▶ Talk about the way street sellers would shout out their wares. Encourage the children to make up a small role-play set in Victorian times, based on a whelk stallholder or a seller of cockles and mussels.

▶ Teach the children the song 'Cockles and mussels'.

Interview: Seaside holidays when I was young

In this interview, Sheila Hogbin talks about her earliest memories of holidays in Abersoch in the 1930s. Her account of how long it seemed to take to travel there will coincide with children's own experiences of going on holiday, as will her memories of the things that she used to do on the beach. Sheila's photographs give a real idea of what her childhood holidays were like – what she wore, and the beach toys she used to play with. We can see in one of them the knitted swimming costume she did not like having to wear. What emerges, however, is that many of the things that children like to do on the beach today have remained the same; it is only the small details that have changed.

Discussing the interview

▶ Can the children remember the name of the place Sheila used to go on holiday when she was young?

▶ How did she get there? How long did the journey take? What games did Sheila play in the car to pass the time? Are they like the games that the children play now?

▶ Can the class remember where Sheila said they used to stop for breaks? Where do the children's families stop for breaks today; what kind of place?

▶ Ask the children how many things they can remember about what Sheila did when she was on the beach.

▶ Can the children remember what Sheila did not like?

▶ Sheila explains what is different about playing on the beach now. What does she mention?

▶ Can they remember what Sheila used to wear on the beach?

Activities

▶ Ask the class to recall the place where Sheila used to go on holiday, and find it on a map of the UK.

▶ Discuss what the children like and do not like about being on the beach nowadays. Working with the whole class, make a list of likes and dislikes. Discuss which are similar to Sheila's likes and dislikes, and which are different.

▶ Ask parents and carers if they can send in some photographs from seaside holidays that the children can use in class. Use these for discussion, in a display, and for the children to write about.

NOTES ON THE PHOTOCOPIABLE PAGES

Word cards   PAGES 69–73

A number of specific types of vocabulary have been introduced on the word cards:

▶ words related to the passing of time and chronology, such as *after the war*, *when my grandparents were young*, *the 1950s*

▶ words to describe geographical features, such as *coast*, *cliff*, *shore*

▶ everyday words associated with the seaside, such as *sun cream*, *bucket*, *spade*

▶ period-specific seaside vocabulary, such as *steam boat*, *bathing machine*.

Encourage the children to think of other appropriate words to add to those provided, in order to build up a word bank for the theme of holidays. They could also use the word cards in displays and to help them in writing captions for their pictures.

Activities
▶ Once you have made copies of the word cards, cut them out and laminate them, and use them as often as possible when talking about holidays or in word games.
▶ Make pairing games with sets of pictures and word cards, getting the children, with support if necessary, to match words and pictures. Make a note of the children who can choose matching words.
▶ Organise times during whole class plenaries to practise reading the word cards together. Follow up this activity with pairs of children reading the words. Check which words each child can read.
▶ Use the word cards in a matching game. Give each child a word from any set of word cards. Read out a word and hold it up. The child with the matching word should hold up his or her card. It could also be played as a team game with points to provide greater motivation.

Timeline showing seaside resorts in the past and today   PAGE 74

This timeline can be used to introduce children to the notion of chronology over a long period of time. No dates have been included, as they may prove confusing for children who have not progressed far in terms of working with large numbers. The timeline is primarily to introduce young children to the idea of a sequence of events, presented in chronological order.

The timeline could be used at the beginning of a topic on seaside holidays in the past, to give children some visual representation of what we mean by *long ago*, *recent* or *today*. This kind of timeline is also useful at the end of a topic, for checking children's success in grasping ideas of sequence and chronology.

Discussing the timeline
▶ At the beginning of the topic, ask the class what they think this timeline shows.
▶ Discuss what we mean by *Victorian*.
▶ What does *Twentieth century* mean? Ask the children to give dates that are part of the twentieth century.
▶ Finally, discuss what *present* or *present day* means.

Activities
▶ Make a large class timeline using this as an example. Ask the children to put in the appropriate places on the timeline any relevant pictures they find, or give them pictures from the CD to use.
▶ Add other periods that you have been studying to the timeline if the children have a good grasp of how it works.

Stories about holidays
These stories and non-fiction texts can be read to the class in story time, or used in shared reading time within the Literacy Hour. The non-fiction texts are intended to be informative as well as providing a different genre of text. The texts could be used to compare features of fiction and non-fiction as part of a literacy lesson.

The stories might be used as a stimulus for shared writing about adventures on the beach or other holiday places. Pictures on the CD relate to the texts and can be used to illustrate them. More able children could be encouraged to make up stories of their own to tell the class. They could form the beginning of a class collection of stories about the beach, the sea or sea adventures.

Saving the starfish   PAGE 75

This story is based on a real occurrence, reported in the news in March 2002. Hundreds of thousands of starfish were washed up on the north Norfolk coast. The creatures were left stranded on the beach at Holkham and many died through drying out. There were so many on this particular occasion, the covering of starfish on the beach was said to resemble a carpet. This is an annual phenomenon, caused by very strong winds disturbing the seabed and dislodging the starfish, which are then washed ashore and are unable to get back to the water quickly enough.

This story can be used to introduce the children to further information about the life of the starfish. It could also be used to involve the children in thinking about the environment and the need to care for living creatures.

Discussing the story

▶ What do the class think the children and their grandparents are doing there on the beach? Has anyone in the class ever been to the seaside for a day?

▶ Talk about how the starfish had got so high up on the beach. Explain that this happens quite often because of stormy weather.

▶ Ask the children why they think the old woman was throwing the starfish back into the sea. Discuss the idea that people can help look after animals and care for them. Ask if the children have ever had the chance of helping an animal.

Activities

▶ Ask the children to look carefully at the story and tell you what the children's names are.

▶ See how many questions they can find in the story.

▶ Make a set of folding, concertina books for the class, each book having spaces for four pictures. Get the children to draw four pictures, each representing a stage of the story. This will assist the children in understanding the idea of chronological sequence.

Starfish PAGE 76

This simple, non-fiction text can be used to introduce children to reading factual material or to give them some experience in reading this type of text. It will probably introduce some new vocabulary, such as *spiny* or *limb*, with which they may need help. You may wish to compare the different types of writing used in the story 'Saving the starfish' and this piece. This will draw children's attention to the difference between fiction and non-fiction writing.

This text gives details about the features of the starfish which can be used in conjunction with discussion about the 'Starfish' picture on the CD.

Discussing the text

▶ What kind of skin does the text say the starfish has? Discuss what *spiny* means. If possible, look at an example of a real starfish to see more clearly the structure of the skin.

▶ Ask if anyone knows what *agile* means. Discuss when a starfish might need to be agile rather than slow in its movements.

▶ See if the children can tell you how it prises open shells. What do they think it does?

▶ Do they know what *suckers* are? Compare these to the suckers on the end of a toy bow and arrow, for example. Discuss how starfish might use suckers.

▶ Explain that a starfish can regrow even if half of its body is broken off.

Activities

▶ Provide some sentence openings about starfish, such as *Starfish can move slowly...* and ask the children, working in pairs, to complete these.

▶ Provide the class with a variety of materials for making some starfish patterns and prints.

▶ Ask the children to draw or paint a starfish, concentrating on one of the features mentioned in the text and making it clear in their picture, for example its having five limbs, or showing the suckers, or how it moves in the water.

Toby on the beach PAGE 77

This story aims to bring alive for children what the beach would have been like in Victorian or Edwardian times. Many features would have been the same, such as the dogs, the people bathing. Some things, however, would have been different, such as the stalls selling winkles and jellied eels, the bathing machines and the Punch and Judy show, which was more common than today. By involving the children in a humorous tale, they will begin to identify more easily with the unusual features of the past that they encounter in the pictures on the CD.

Discussing the story

▶ Ask the children who the main character is in this story. What is his name and what is he?

▶ Why do they think Toby runs away from his family?

▶ Ask for volunteers to recall all the incidents he is involved in. See if they can relate the incidents in the right order.
▶ Talk about the dogs that the children may have at home, mentioning their names and the things they get up to.

Activities
▶ Get the children to produce large paintings of Toby on the beach.
▶ In a shared writing session, ask the children for an idea for another incident involving Toby, and let them complete the story while working in pairs.
▶ Discuss the kind of things Toby might do on a beach today, for example he may get mixed up in a volleyball game, or swim out to sea following a jet-ski.

The scallop shell PAGE 78

This non-fiction text is intended to challenge very able readers. It contains a considerable amount of factual information, much of which will need explanation, including terms like *British Isles* and *100 metres*. A collection of real scallop shells would enable the children to follow the description more easily, by identifying the features of the shell that they hear or read about.

Discussing the text
▶ Ask the children where scallops like to live. Explain that there are many different kinds of scallops that live in different parts of the world.
▶ Ask why the children think the scallop is described as looking like a fan.
▶ Discuss what *souvenir* means. Ask what kind of things the children have seen that are made from shells, such as small ornaments, soap dishes, ashtrays.

Activities
▶ Use the 'Shell' picture on the CD to accompany the reading of this text. If possible, use a collection of real shells for the children to handle.
▶ Look at a map of Britain with the class and discuss where the scallop shells are found, just off the coasts.
▶ Challenge the children to use the scallop design to make a regular, repeated pattern to go round a plate. They could make a simple block print to make their pattern.

Writing/drawing frames
These vary in difficulty, from opportunities for drawing for less able readers and writers, to more demanding tasks for the more able. Nevertheless, less able writers could be assisted to complete the more difficult writing frames by support from an adult, or perhaps by working as a pair with a more able reader and writer.

Old and new holidays PAGE 79

This sheet could be used at the end of a lesson where there has been discussion about the similarities and differences between holidays in the past and holidays today. It will be helpful to have modelled on the board how to note comparisons as discussion takes place. The use of a word bank will have helped the children to become familiar with the vocabulary they will need to use in completing the chart. Children could draw in the chart if they find the vocabulary or writing difficult.

My favourite holiday PAGE 80

This writing frame is intended for very able readers and writers, who may need some extension tasks. It will need to be discussed before the children work on it alone or in pairs, and perhaps the first sentence could be modelled for them. Children should be encouraged to use their word books or word banks to help them complete the sentences. The word cards on photocopiable pages 71–3 could also be used.

Time word cards

long ago

when my parents/carers were young

when my grandparents were young

after the war

the 1930s, 1940s, 1950s, 1960s

Time-sequencing word cards

recent

modern

old

oldest

new

newest

coast

sand

cliff

beach

shingle

shore

sandcastle

sun cream

swimsuit

seashells

bucket

spade

steam boat

Punch and Judy show

pier

steam train

amusement arcade

bathing machine

From left to right, by kind permission of Brighton and Hove Local Studies Library,
© Brighton and Hove Visitor and Convention Bureau

Timeline showing seaside resorts in the past and today

Victorian times

Twentieth century

Present day

SCHOLASTIC
PHOTOCOPIABLE

Saving the starfish

Razia and her brother Assim had been taken to the beach for the day by their grandparents as a treat. They were playing on the beach when they saw an old woman bending down, carefully collecting things. They asked their grandparents if they could go and see what was happening. As they got nearer, they saw that where the old woman stood, the beach was covered with lovely starfish.

"I wonder why all these starfish are on the beach instead of in the water," said Razia.

"I don't know," said Assim. "Something must be wrong."

The children went closer and saw that the old woman was carefully collecting up as many starfish as she could carry, and then throwing them back into the water.

"Why are you doing that?" asked Assim.

"Well, if I don't they will get too dry and die," said the old woman. They have been washed up on the sand by strong wind and waves and they will die if they cannot get back into the water."

"Oh," said the children. "Can we help?"

"Of course," said the old woman. So Razia and Assim called their grandparents over and they all worked hard until the sun went down. They saved hundreds of starfish that day.

© Image Club

Many starfish have a hard spiny skin. They have five limbs or legs. They move slowly, but are strong and can be agile when they need to be. They can turn themselves the right way up if they are turned over in the water. They can open sea shells with their limbs. Starfish have hundreds of tiny feet on their limbs which are like suckers. If starfish have a limb broken off, they are able to grow a new one.

Toby on the beach

Toby the dog was at the seaside. He was there with his family for the day. Toby loved the sands and the water. He liked to dig deep holes in the sand and splash in the waves.

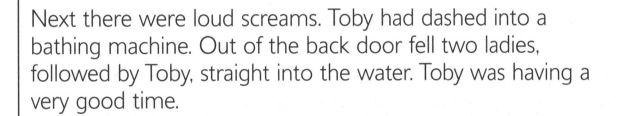

Later in the day it grew very hot. His family were tired and Toby got bored. He decided to go and explore on his own. Off he ran down the beach, but he did not look where he was going. Crash! Toby had knocked into a stall selling winkles and jellied eels. They fell all over the beach, but Toby ran on.

Next there were loud screams. Toby had dashed into a bathing machine. Out of the back door fell two ladies, followed by Toby, straight into the water. Toby was having a very good time.

Then he heard loud voices and children laughing. It was a Punch and Judy show, but who was that silly dog with a frill round its neck?

"I'm Toby," said the strange dog.
"No you're not, I'm Toby!" said Toby.

There was a lot of barking and yapping as the dogs began to fight. The children all began to shout and scream. The Punch and Judy man was getting angry.

"Here you are, Toby!" said a familiar voice.
"Oh, thank goodness," thought Toby. "It's my family again."

Toby was glad to go back to his own safe spot on the beach.

The scallop shell

The scallop is a sea animal with a very strong shell. It is found on the coasts of the British Isles. Scallops like to live about 100 metres from the shore in the water. They stay in hollows in the sand on the seabed.

The scallop shell is shaped like a fan. It has grooves, and is thick and solid. It is often used to make souvenirs. Buildings in ancient Roman times were sometimes decorated with scallop shell shapes.

Scallops have tentacles inside the shell, which they use to get food. They can open and close the two halves of their shell when they want to move around or search for food.

Scallops are good swimmers. They glide through the water and over the seabed by snapping their shells together. They can also squirt water at other animals.

📖 SCHOLASTIC
PHOTOCOPIABLE

Old and new holidays

▷ Make a list of the things that are the same and different about the pictures of a holiday a long time ago and a present-day holiday at the seaside.

Things that are the same	Things that are different

My favourite holiday

△ Finish the sentences that have been started for you below:

I like to go to the seaside because

_____

At the seaside I like to play with

_____

I like to play on the beach because

_____

I like to play in the water because

_____

Remember to put full stops at the end of each sentence.